FLATPACK DEM

POWER TOOLS FOR RECLAIMING LOCAL POLITICS

BY

PETER MACFADYEN

ADDITIONAL TEXT BY PETER ANDREWS

'FOR ALF'

eco-logic books

First published in 2019 by eco-logic books
www.eco-logicbooks.com
Updated and reprinted in 2020

ISBN 978 1899233 27 4

Cover Design   Sammy Hayward   srhillustration.com
based on an original idea by Matt Welsted   thedraughtsman.me
Book Design: Steve Palmer   stevejp56@gmail.com
Editing: Jessica Andrews   jessicakatherineandrews.com
Printed & bound: 4edge, Hockley, Essex

Further copies of this book may be bought from eco-logic books. We would
welcome enquiries for bulk orders of this book from independent local
groups.

Extract from the Minutes of the Finance & Policy Committee Extraordinary Meeting

Held on Tuesday 11th June 2019 at 6pm in The Mayor's Parlour, The Shire Hall, Monmouth

69. Sponsorship Policy

b) To consider offer from Mr C B*** of free of charge bottles of pasteurised apple juice (produced from home) – on condition the council does not buy any cartons of soft drinks.

Cllr J*** left room – declared personal and prejudicial interest.

The offer was welcomed. As only apple juice would be available Cllr W*** said this was too constrained a choice. Cllr F*** stated that the juice must be proven as fit for human consumption and required suitable certification before supply to MTC.

Proposal: Respond to Mr. B*** that the offer, while welcome, must be unconditional and only accepted if suitable certification provided.

Proposed: F*** Sec: C***

Unanimous.

On 22 April 2019 *The Telegraph* reported that 130 out of 163 parishes in Dorset have not attracted enough candidates to hold elections on May 2, while 20 have no candidates at all, so will no longer function – the picture seems similar in other areas across the country.

Contents

1. Flatpackery, or why politics needs to be reclaimed by the people... and how to do it

"Don't bother to lobby your local councillor – become one."

This is a book about reclaiming politics. Anyone, anywhere engaging in the decisions that affect their life is involved in politics. And real engagement, it turns out, is vital for everyone, both for our personal health and that of our communities and, as I will argue, for the future of humanity.

In 2014 I wrote a book called *Flatpack Democracy – a guide to creating independent politics.* 'Flatpack' described the idea that you could open the book, take out the pieces and easily assemble democracy at community level. The book set out a method of taking political power at the parish or town levels. It told the story of what happened in Frome, a market town in south west England, where in 2011 ten of us did indeed get elected, and inadvertently ended up running Frome Town Council.

Why was that story worth telling? Because as Independents for Frome (IfF) we worked together and campaigned on a set of values, rather than on a traditional manifesto that would have set out what we would do if elected. This allowed us to create a much more focussed and ambitious programme that put Frome first, rather than any personal or party political ambitions. What Frome achieved has attracted significant attention and interest. This is especially relevant as it has happened at a time when the lack of government funding has seen a huge reduction in local services and community-level activity.

Flatpack Democracy 2.0 takes us through the second independent-led council of 2015-19 and ends with the results of the 2019 election campaign. It sets out what has been achieved, how we went about it and some ideas for the future. It also learns from the experiences of others who used the first book to take power at a local level. Over this period I've seen interest in politics and trust in politicians collapse, with democracy increasingly being seen by the public as dysfunctional and irrelevant. Frome's achievements feed into a real hunger to rebuild trust in democracy and reconnect people to power.

When ideas take off, there's often a risk they'll attract undue attention and be replicated unsuccessfully because a more nuanced and critical approach was required. This is especially true for some of the ideas in Flatpack Democracy, particularly in relation to whether they can be applied at different levels of local government and in different countries with different electoral systems. Flatpack Democracy 2.0, based as it is on a whole new range of experiences, addresses some of those issues.

Standing as councillors in the 2011 Frome Town Council elections was not part of a carefully thought through plan. We saw an opportunity to change things for the good in our community, and believed the process might be challenging and fun too. As our ideas developed and the world around us changed, a general direction and ethos emerged and evolved. We haven't developed a blueprint that can be slavishly copied but rather ideas and experience on which others can build.

At a talk in Holland I was asked about the 'political theory of Flatpackery'. Hearing the term 'Flatpackery' was both exciting and humbling; that someone could create this new word in a language that wasn't their own is remarkable! There is also a Flatcap party in Yorkshire, and I'm not sure if Flapjack Democracy is a positive evolution. If you become part of this experiment in new ways of doing local democracy, I would love to hear from you about what works and what doesn't.

Peter Macfadyen
www.flatpackdemocracy.co.uk
@flatpackdemoc

2. Frome's politics:
what's all the fuss been about?

Frome Town Council Mayor and ex Mayors celebrating the 2015 election results

Introduction

The vast majority of people in Britain have never had any significant say in what happens around them, the things that significantly affect their lives. This really matters when the tiny minority who do hold all the power fail to create an environment in which the disempowered can thrive. A short time spent in Accident and Emergency or a look at our response to climate change should convince you of that.

Although I'd spent all my adult life in social activism, my experiences as a councillor bought home to me the shocking state of our so-called democracy. *Flatpack Democracy* was an attempt to express ideas as to how this might change.

Just in case you haven't read *Flatpack Democracy*, it's the story of how a bunch of ardently non-political party people went from moaning in a pub to running Frome Town Council, following an upbeat and unorthodox election campaign. What made *Flatpack Democracy* interesting to so many people was that it presented more than just an idea of how to do things differently; it was an account of real life, featuring real people, getting real things done.

For context, here are some basic facts about Frome. It's the fourth largest town in the county of Somerset and largest in the district of Mendip. Frome's Town Council is one of the biggest of roughly 9,000 councils in England and has a budget of around £1.3 million. As such, it represents the basic building block of democracy in our country. Although outwardly attractive and prosperous, Frome, like much of rural England, also has areas of considerable deprivation. The industries that formed the basis of Frome's wealth in the last century have all now gone; three out of four of the businesses in the town have less than five employees.

The three factors that made 2011 the right moment for Independents For Frome (IfF) to emerge

If you read the next section it may look like we'd carefully analysed the political situation and designed a strategy to take Frome into the sunlit uplands of local-government nirvana. That was definitely not the case: all we knew then was we wanted a radical change in the way Frome was run.

Our initial question was 'could IfF remove party politics and create an ambitious, effective town council that was accessible to everyone?' My own personal question was 'could we do this in a way in which the voluntary job of councillor was both enjoyable and used my skills and experience well?'

We identified three opportunities to begin to bring about that (r)evolution.

1) Problems of party politics

Frome had traditionally elected its councillors along party political lines. In other words, candidates were drawn from the tiny numbers of local party members and presented to the electorate pretty much as 'Mrs Jones, Green Party', with no further information. Once elected, the party groups then tended to vote against each other, mirroring the political system of Westminster. Party ideology often guided their decisions rather than what was best at a local level.

Our new group of Independents for Frome (IfF) felt this was fundamentally wrong, in part because the way it works is rooted in what's called 'Representative Democracy'. This means that we elect someone to represent us and make the decisions they feel are best for us. Every four or five years we, the public, get a chance to review who we'd like as our representative. In the years in between elections, we get virtually no chance to influence the way things go.

Not that many years ago, when communication was difficult – think quills and horses – this made some sense. Now – think emails and Twitter – engagement at all levels of decision-making is much easier. In addition, the kind of decisions we ask our representatives to make seem to be getting increasingly complex. The newly formed IfF recognised that a small group of councillors could not possibly have the experience and skills to make good decisions all the time. Therefore, it was obvious we needed to change the model to one that really engaged with, and used, the wisdom and potential of the community. In other words, everyone has something to contribute.

I would argue that political parties have never been useful at a town and parish council level. In fact, many places do not have councillors elected on a party basis.

2) The Localism Act

Even for those of us stuck in the bubble of politics, it can be hard to remember that David Cameron's other big idea was the 2011 Localism Act. He summed it up by saying, 'I believe the central objective of the new politics we need should be a massive, sweeping, radical redistribution of power... we must take power from the elite and hand it to the man and woman in the street...' Every party generally vows to do the same, but this time it was actually enshrined in an Act of Parliament.

Amongst the initial IfF group, Mel Usher, along with colleagues who had worked in local government, knew there was an intention to move power downwards. Historically, parish and town councils, like Frome, did very little beyond looking after the park, commenting on planning decisions made elsewhere and a fair bit of mayoral swaggering about in gold chains. The Localism Act promised much more. Radically, it said that if the town clerk had the right qualifications, then the council could agree to do anything that wasn't illegal. It could borrow money, support and run its own commercial projects, buy back land and buildings previously lost to the town and take on all kinds of services never before tackled at this level. The newly formed IfF recognised that the Localism Act meant that we, as new councillors, had scope for a much more interesting and productive role; it gave us the potential to really get things done, way beyond looking after the park.

3) Austerity

The austerity policy that Conservative and coalition governments have followed since the financial crisis of 2007/8 has the supposed aim of controlling the national debt by reducing public spending. It also aims to shrink the role of the welfare state and at the same time keep taxes low to ensure growth. The key impact of this policy for Frome Town Council has been the reduction in money it's had for spending on public works. Grants from central government to the county and district have been massively cut. And because they've not been allowed to increase their income from council tax above a limited percentage, it's meant reducing statutory services to the minimum and completely cutting everything else.

At the start of IfF's management of Frome's council, Mel Usher was already saying 'if we don't do it ourselves, it won't happen'. It took me longer to realise the full impact austerity would have, and seven years later, austerity is really biting. Early casualties were cuts to both grants and staff funding for the arts, sport and youth work. Now even the core services, like care for the elderly, disabled and special educational facilities, are suffering. Over and above these obvious losses, the lack of capacity of the district and county council to make simple planning decisions, transfer land or respond to pretty much any request for help has had a paralysing effect on local government in general.

Given this, the only route open to Frome has been to invent new ways to provide services or bring in funding. I'll go on to look at this in more detail in Chapters 4 and 5.

What is IfF and what makes it different?

The following is a summary of what Councillor Toby Eliot said about IfF at one of the joint staff/councillor meetings we've arranged: *"IfF as an organisation doesn't really exist outside of an election. It is a framework to get good, independent people elected. Elected councillors are the custodians of the 'brand'.*

We shape what is to be the focus and decide how we work together. We came together as a group of individuals. There is no written ethos agreed by the group of IfF councillors. What we do have is published election material which says what we said we'd do before we were voted in, the IfF Ways of Working (how we work with each other) and the agreed Town Council Strategy."

However, we are officially registered with the Electoral Commission as a minor political party and there are two key reasons why I personally regarded it as essential to form an official group.

Firstly, most people seem averse to change and wary of the unknown. This makes it a real challenge for anyone outside the established political parties to get elected. The vast majority of people vote as they've always voted. In addition, parties have the experience of how to win elections, together with the funds and person-power to run a campaign.

So IfF has had to develop the basics of a campaign strategy that allows a disparate group to work together. Crucially, these individuals don't have to agree on what they will do if elected, on single issues, broader policy or strategy, or even where they come from in terms of traditional party political views. However, to get elected they needed to work together. In addition, during the initial stages of running a council, acting as a group for procedural decisions is crucial. For example, the largest 'group' gets to choose the chair of the council, and individual independents are not a group.

Secondly, the level of flexibility outlined above comes with ambiguity and there must be limits to the level of diversity with which a group can cope. (I'll come on to how these have been tested later.) My experience elsewhere shows that a group of independent councillors are capable of flying off in every direction and unlikely to focus on the challenges needed to overcome significant issues like austerity or take on climate change. They will tend to form into subgroups and cliques, and the politics of all that takes away energy that could be directed towards common goals. In order to realise ambitious achievements, there needs to be a common direction. Thus IfF have established some core elements as rocks onto which our councillors can anchor themselves.

The Ways of Working

In my view, the Ways of Working are the key to our success and the main difference between IfF and a traditional independent group. They were established at the start of IfF, then updated by the 2015 councillors (see Appendix 1). There are five core principles: independence, integrity, positivity, creativity and respect. A key criterion for the selection of an IfF candidate is their commitment to our Ways of Working. Crucially, these are underpinned by 10 specific ways we challenge ourselves to act:

- Avoid identifying ourselves so personally with a particular poistion that it excludes constructive debate.
- Be prepared to be swayed by the arguments of others and admitting mistakes.

- Be willing and able to participate in rational debate leading to a conclusion.
- Understand the value of constructive debate.
- Accept that you win some, you lose some; it's usually nothing personal and there's really no point in taking defeats to heart.
- Maintain confidentially where requested and agree when it will be expected.
- Share leadership and responsibility and take time to communicate the intention of, and the approach to, the work we undertake.
- Have confidence in, and adhere to, the mechanisms and processes of decision-making that we establish, accepting that the decisions of the majority are paramount.
- Sustain an intention to involve each other and others rather than working in isolation.
- Trust and have confidence and optimism in other people's expertise, knowledge and intentions. Talk to each other not about each other.

It's these specific areas of intent that move an IfF-led council into new areas of politics. Although they're intended for the group, there's generally acceptance that it's good practice to apply these principles to our relationship with staff as well.

Ambition

The cultural anthropologist Margaret Mead is credited with saying: "We are continually faced with great opportunities which are brilliantly disguised as unsolvable problems" and also, "If the future is to remain open and free, we need people who can tolerate the unknown, who will not need the support of completely worked out systems of traditions or blueprints from the past."

Lack of ambition is often cited as the reason why greater things are not achieved at parish and town council level. I've heard it said that what happens in town councils goes largely unnoticed – usually because there isn't much to notice.

As an aside, I was in a small city near here recently and the newly co-opted independent councillor told me his first meeting had an agenda with three items. First, was his co-option. Second, was a very long discussion on the need for a second portrait of the Queen. And third, another long discussion on whether it's appropriate for the deputy mayor to attend twinning events in the absence of the mayor.
So the starting point is often low, but with a degree of ambition and the courage to take risks there's the potential to achieve a great deal.

Thinking big

Despite being 'just' a town council, the basic level of government, there's a real sense within IfF, and indeed within Frome, that we are a 'can do' town and that many things can happen through creative use of resources, commitment and determination. Whilst we don't try to provide statutory services, we do find ways to combat austerity through improving communications between the statutory and voluntary sector, by enabling and kick-starting community-led initiatives and by harnessing and bringing together local resources in surprising ways. Frome and IfF show a level of confidence that things can change and a belief that local people can make a difference.

We don't limit our thinking, we 'think big' and we pragmatically seize opportunities as they present themselves; above all, we think long term.

Taking risks

Alongside big thinking comes taking risks. Former Frome councillor and local government expert Mel Usher is right when he says 'we won't kill anyone'. Providing you make decisions in an open way, using the information you have at the time whilst accepting you might not succeed, then taking risks is usually a good idea. Failure to take risks would lead us back to where IfF started in 2011. When IfF took over the council they inherited large cash reserves simply because the previous councillors hadn't taken any chances – and thus had done very little.

Doing what's best for Frome

One of the things that really underpins how we work together as councillors is our sense of common purpose: we all want to do our best for Frome. Whilst there are many examples of particular councillors feeling strongly about certain issues and that they're 'right', the central motivation that drives us all is 'how can we make Frome a great place to live, work and visit, and sustain all that into the future?' This sense of purpose brings together a very diverse set of projects, initiatives, interests and actions.

A shared vision: equality, prosperity and a sustainable future

Another important thing we do is focus on equality and fairness. No councillor wants Frome to be successful for some parts of society and not others, or for Frome to succeed without due regard to the environment or in the longer term.

Some councillors focus on health and wellbeing; others focus on increasing opportunities for employment and the sustainability of small businesses; and yet others have a focus on energy efficiency, reduction of waste and pollution. These work together to give all Frome's residents the same resources and opportunities to thrive.

Shared values: participation, empowerment and leadership

In embracing participation, we've not been blind to the importance of leadership, passion and sponsorship. We want to work with the town. We want to support and help to bring together the many groups and individuals already doing great things. We want to listen and involve people in what we do and how we do it. However, the issue of participation is interesting. When and on what issues do we ask for views and use those to make decisions? On what issues do we leave the voting to the public?

How we navigate the nuance and complexity of participation, yet maintain leadership is an issue that keeps us on our toes and leads to experimentation, diversity of approach and regular debate.

Embracing diversity

As a group of councillors, we are quite diverse; indeed, we were selected to cover a wide range of ages, backgrounds and interests. There's a tolerance of members' diversity, approaches and interests, and of the amount of available time to give. Each councillor has, over time, found their own niche and ways of engaging with the process of governing. There are committees, panels, project sponsors and advisory groups to join. We meet as a group of councillors each month to discuss important issues, think about the future and reflect on how we're working. We have occasional weekends away together to reflect on how we're doing and what needs to change.

The structures we experiment with allow us to work in partnership with the staff in a way that reflects skills and interests, within both the staff and councillor group. One of the ironies of the council structure, or lack of it, is that elected councillors, being the custodians of the IfF 'brand', shape their focus and decide how to work together. Thus, how the current 2019 crop of councillors behave, and where their priorities will lie, is entirely up to them. And as everyone knows, past performance is no guarantee of future results.

3. The 2015 and 2019 elections

Ideas for Frome

For the last eight years IfF have done their best to make Frome even better for everyone who lives and works here. But there is still a lot more to be done.

We've attracted nearly a million pounds worth of investment into community projects, and we will continue to bid for grant money while still balancing the books.

Our goal is that as much money as possible is spent back into the local community, creating growth and opportunities for everyone in an inclusive town. As a Council, we will use local firms for our contracts wherever possible and will encourage other local businesses to do the same.

The people of Frome have had a big input into where the town's money is spent and what our future priorities should be. We will hold more participatory events so that everyone can continue to have their say.

A wide range of community groups across the town are supported by the Council. In the next four years we are particularly keen to work with groups focussing on young people's mental health and which bring young and old together.

With the Neighbourhood Plan in place, any future developments must meet the needs of the whole community. As well as having input ourselves, we will back residents to engage directly with developers and have their voice heard.

For a cleaner, healthier town, we will take measures to improve air quality. We will back greener travel options, continue to support energy efficiency and renewables, and work with local communities to reduce waste and make recycling easier.

Our parks and green spaces are essential to the town and should be accessible for everyone. We want to encourage community gardening wherever we can and as a priority we will be looking for more allotment land.

Vote IfF on May 2nd

facebook.com/IndependentsforFrome
@If_Frome
iffrome.org.uk

I'M FOR FROME iff

Introduction

This chapter covers the 2015 and 2019 Frome Town Council elections. I'll look at 2015 in detail and pick up on key things done differently and new learnings from 2019. This section adds to the experiences of the 2011 elections covered in Chapters 7 to 10 of Flatpack Democracy. It provides a good story of two elections with extraordinary results and a lot of nerdy stuff for people engaged in local election campaigns.

Background to the 2015 campaign

IfF headed into the May 2015 elections in a completely different position from 2011. We had a high profile council that had clearly achieved a lot for the town and plenty of energy bubbling over from our previous efforts. In my naivety, I thought the political parties would focus on the district and county elections, leaving IfF to carry on doing a good job in Frome. How wrong I was!

In the end, there were 49 candidates for the 17 seats, showing, if nothing else, what IfF has done for local choice. There was a clear desire by the parties to regain what they saw as their rightful place as rulers of Frome. It was always going to be about power, not quality of candidates, governance or anything else.

None of the parties had enough candidates for every ward, which is often a crucial factor for independent groups, who can pick up party votes where there is no candidate for that party.

The Greens chose not to stand at the town level. They rightly identified the risk of undermining IfF's huge progress in environmental areas. They focused on the district instead and won three seats there for the first time ever. There was some discussion of a semi-formal pact of support for the Greens' district campaign, but IfF does not exist as a decision-making party in the traditional sense so could not agree to such a deal, even if it were felt to be advantageous. Some of us gave informal personal support to their district campaign without impacting on any rules or the views of other IfF candidates.

In 2015 there were national and district elections on the same day as ours; this raised fears that, as so often happens, people would vote along party lines. We weren't sure whether a higher turnout, because of the national election, would help or hinder us. Neither could we predict what the effects of a resurgent UKIP alongside the predicted LibDem meltdown would be.

Faced with the prospect of endless uninformed speculation on these issues, we basically decided to ignore them all and go for as many votes as possible. National parties have computer-aided lists and printouts of registered voters and supporters to aid their campaigns, but we've never got excited by such things. It takes too much time and organisation trying to work out who might do what.

After winning all the seats in 2015, the background to the third 2019 election campaign was different again.

Background to the 2019 campaign

While there was a sense that the IfF was still broadly popular, some of our high-profile decisions hadn't been too well received. Perhaps IfF had become the reviled establishment? Perhaps we were now being seen as simply 'politicians'?

This time the Lib Dems joined the Greens in not standing 'because IfF has done such a fantastic job'. Two Lib Dems revolted against this edict and stood as unallied independents while also standing as Lib Dems in the district elections. There was one 'Real Independent', who never revealed exactly what that meant; the Tories managed only two candidates; and Labour put up 14 candidates out of a possible 17 seats. Apparently all local Labour parties are under central office instruction to compete wherever possible. There were elections for every seat, but this overall lack of competition is a concern given IfF's initial desire to raise interest and engagement in local democracy.

There was only a Mendip district election on the same day, so we expected turnout to be much lower than in 2015.

The key difference between the two campaigns was that while 2015 was run by the candidates with the help of a few key supporters, in 2019 four non-candidates ran the campaign with steadily increasing involvement of the wider group.

Registration and some technical stuff before you start your election campaign

IfF nearly didn't make it onto the ballot paper in 2015. We'd not re-registered as a minor political party, which meant that as things stood we couldn't appear under the IfF banner on the ballot paper. Fortunately, this problem was easily rectified. 'Someone' should have remembered, but this a good example of where having no administrative structure between elections has its weaknesses.

Despite this experience, a similar mistake was made in 2019, eventually leading to no IfF emblems appearing on the ballot papers. Had there been more independents competing, this could have had serious consequences; as each candidate's name had 'Independents for Frome' after it, it luckily did not. You're allowed up to six words next to your name on the ballot paper, so it probably wouldn't have been terminal anyway.

Elsewhere I've discussed the advantages and disadvantages of registering as a political party, but to be clear, I wanted to list the three main advantages:

1) It allows the group to have a recognised emblem that appears on the ballot paper.
2) To be recognised as a group once elected. This is important as the makeup of committee members on a council is often decided by the size of a group or party. This then leads to the potential to elect the chair from your group, which can be a major advantage.
3) With a larger number of people on the case, you're less likely to miss deadlines and make silly mistakes – at least, in theory!

New groups who wish to register need to know that initial registering with the Electoral Commission can take up to three months. Groups that want to stand at district or other levels must take all this a step further by registering as a political party. This may take even longer, with even more bureaucracy to negotiate.

Key dates

Having sorted out the registration, the next step is to get some key dates in place. The two most important of these are 1) when candidates must be registered by and 2) when postal votes are sent out.

In 2015 IfF was lucky enough to have the same agent as in 2011 to help with the paperwork, making sure the forms were filled out correctly and taken to the returning officer at the district council on time. A new supporter took on that role in 2019. The agent is ideally someone who is well organised and prepared to constantly remind, cajole and even bully. The returning officer has always been really helpful in talking us through the dates and process, all of which is laid out in plain English on the web, including that vital date when candidates must be registered by, which is about four weeks before election day.

Postal and proxy votes

The postal vote date is a less obvious hurdle to fall at. We were more aware of it in the 2015 election, in part because of a snafu in an earlier by-election when we found ourselves delivering leaflets only to be met with 'thanks, but I've already voted'. Previous experience, however, counted for nothing in 2019. Despite all the spreadsheets and reminders, in some wards the relevant leaflet went out a few days after the postal vote had arrived. Don't make the same mistake.

The proportion of people using postal votes rises in each election. This is in part because having asked for a postal vote once it stays that way, unless you deliberately change it.

Around 17% of voters now use postal votes for the general election in Frome – and in 2015 this was probably the same for the town. For some inexplicable reason the numbers of postal voters varies hugely around the country, with somewhere near Sunderland clocking up 43% last time and a constituency in Birmingham managing only 7%.

In addition, more people who have postal votes actually vote. In the 2015 election 86% of postal voters voted, compared to 63% of those voting on the day at a polling station. I can't find research to prove it, but I suspect postal voters are predominantly older and more likely to be conservative (with a large and small C).

Soon after the postal vote hits the mat, I think it's best to assume people will fill it in and post it off. The friendly returning officer will probably tell you when the date is going to be, but two weeks before election day is a good starting point. Make sure you get to people in time.

Voter registration

Another key date is when people need to have registered to vote, or have asked for proxy or postal votes. In every election IfF has had a particular focus on voter registration as a campaign: 'We think you should vote and here's how to register'. It's a great thing to do because it's important for democracy, and as a campaign tool it's very unthreatening. This extends logically into supporting people to get a postal or proxy vote when they might otherwise not take part.

All IfF communication has aimed to increase the numbers of people voting, through voter registration, postal and proxy votes. In 2015, this linked to IfF through the slogan: 'You can vote for whoever you like in national and district elections, but I'm for Frome.'

Only around 55% of 18-19 year olds voted in the last general election, compared to 80% of those over 60. IfF's logic was that we needed to focus on younger people, who are more likely to want to see change and thus vote for something different. For evidence, you only have to look at how in the last election the Labour Party significantly increased their vote by attracting and registering young people. However, registering younger voters is only half the battle, and the youth vote will be much lower in local elections unless you can find specific ways to inspire them to engage. As well as new younger voters with no IfF history, in Frome we also had a very significant number of new households. These newcomers were likely to be both unregistered in Frome and have no idea of our political history, so approaching them required some careful targeting.

Why did all this matter? Because in parish/town elections there's often a low turnout, and thus winning can depend on a tiny number of votes. In 2011 one of our councillors won by a single vote, and in 2015 the tightest margin was still only 14 votes. In Monmouth, independent Rachel Jupp missed winning a bye-election by just two votes. As you can see, every vote really does count!

The candidates

Political parties choose their candidates from party members, theoretically using a set of criteria related to their competence, but all too often based solely on a willingness to stand. The majority of traditional independent candidates are probably people who, in one way or another, don't fit the party model. This may be positive in that they genuinely feel they can do a better job using their experience and will better listen to those who vote for them; however, it's more often negative. They become independents because they've fallen out with their previous party, have extreme views which don't fit with any party or group, or simply feel they have more chance of being elected if not associated with one of our current parties.

The IfF process is radically different as it needs to find candidates who are looking to work as a group, heading in an agreed positive direction.

Attracting candidates

In 2019 we relied heavily on social media and personal contacts to encourage candidates to come forward. IfF Facebook followers have grown from around 1,000 to 1,700 between the two elections. Most of the councillors have their own active sites too, alongside some Twittering. The IfF Facebook posts steered people to the website, which included an expanded FAQ on being a councillor. The website was rebuilt for 2019 but remains relatively simple. Its aim is to set out clearly how IfF is different and to provide information about candidates; this is something lacking for most political party candidates, who rarely get beyond a name and some national ideology.

In 2015 we took out an advert in the local paper to start the process of letting people know there would be an election and to advertise two meetings. In 2019 this was done through social media only. In both cases a series of informal meetings were then held, which were open to all. This enabled people to come and learn more about IfF and the role of councillor. In both years there was contact with around 50 people, with half then completing the full process of applying to stand.

The challenge is inevitably to reach people who believe they are 'not the councillor type' or 'not IfF people'. A significant number of IfF's potential candidates came from one-to-one conversations that encouraged them to see the opportunities, not the problems.

CHOOSING CANDIDATES

In the 2011 elections, roughly the right number of people offered to stand. In 2015 and 2019, a more rigorous process was needed to choose 17 candidates from the 25 or so seriously interested people.

2015 selection process

For the 2015 elections a self-selected group of interested, existing councillors set the broad criteria for the selection committee, and then left them get on with it.

Councillors played no part in the design of the selection process, how it was implemented, or the decisions it came to. (At least, that was the plan, but see below.) The broad criteria were a balanced mix in terms of gender, age, length of residence in Frome, interests and skills, plus a clear understanding of the underlying principles of IfF. Each candidate was asked to write up to two pages covering four simple questions:

- When and why did you move to Frome?
- Why would you want to be a Frome Town Councillor?
- What are your interests and expertise?
- Can you commit to the current IfF Ways of Working?

This aimed to tease out their real motivation for standing, what they would bring to the council, whether they would have the time and commitment, and, crucially, whether they had taken on board the Ways of Working.

There then followed a workshop in two parts. In the first, tables of applicants and some existing councillors discussed what the current council had achieved, what they could have done better and challenges for the future. The groups then fed back and there was some further discussion. The selection panel observed the whole process. This was followed by a full group activity, that discussed the danger that some of Frome's communities might feel excluded by recent developments and looked at what could be done to meet this challenge. These activities aimed to draw out how confident people were, alongside how they handled different situations. In 2015, the person who chaired the panel provided feedback on the selection process summarised below:

- The selection panel needs to be well enough prepared to perform the role so that existing councillors and main supporters are happy to accept their decisions
- In encouraging candidates, it's important to make clear that the panel makes the final selection, and so there can be no promises – implicit or explicit
- Women are more likely to need to be asked to stand as councillors
- Existing councillors should not comment on any applicants to the panel. The exception to this was a current councillor we invited to sit on the panel who was not standing again. He also happened to be a younger person
- The final panel member was someone with no previous involvement in local politics who proved particularly useful
- A procedure needs to be put in place to appoint a replacement should a candidate withdraw.

The feedback noted an element of interference, when an existing councillor felt unhappy that someone was not taken through to the full selection. The same kind of problem emerged in 2019, causing some very challenging dynamics. Where interference is by an existing councillor standing again, it would make sense for this to invalidate them standing. Ultimately, it comes back to an issue of trust and good behaviour. Having tasked the selection group to run the process, it is hugely unhelpful to interfere with their work.

2019 selection process

In 2019 we again asked a small group of people to run the process and make the choices. The group consisted of five people well steeped in IfF's aims and values, including an ex-councillor and someone with a bit of distance from it all. They were effectively commissioned by IfF to choose the candidates. Crucially, past councillors wanting to stand again needed to re-apply and were treated the same as newcomers. In 2015 the selection panel decided that having previously been a councillor was such a significant plus that the six who wanted to re-stand were selected. Personally, I'd have liked to see this subjected to more rigour, as it was for the four who wanted to stand again in 2019. I am delighted none of the very first IfF councillors stood again in 2019, as I believe councillors need to step aside after eight years, to let new ideas and energy flow in.

By 2019 the panel had settled upon a much tighter set of criteria:
- **Diversity**. An awareness and ability to accept and respect others as they are and to work to promote equality of opportunity for the whole community
- **Flexibility.** An ability to strike a balance between your own views and those of others to create a coherent and united group as far as possible
- **Creativity**. The ability to invent innovative solutions to challenging issues
- **Electability**. Having good communication skills and possibly a history of activity that makes you well known and regarded
- **Activity**. A history of active involvement in Frome Town Council or community groups
- **Potency**. A track record in which you have led the delivery of something that has resulted in better outcomes for people
- **Durability**. An ability to operate in the public eye and be responsible and resilient in the face of difficult decisions
- **Clarity**. A good idea of what you would do as a councillor to deliver benefits to the Frome community
- **Integrity**. Adherence to the Nolan principles of public service. (The 7 Nolan Principles were established in 1994 primarily to contain abuse of power by those in public office.)
- **Availability**. A willingness and ability to dedicate adequate time to fulfil the role.

The actual process consisted of a series of activities carried out over a day, involving all the candidates. The process aimed to put candidates in a position of needing to think about the benefits and risks for the town, moving beyond their own personal interests and concerns. For example, they were asked how to handle the public relations of a particularly contentious planning application.

This was followed up over the next few days with one-to-one interviews for some candidates. The panel then selected the final list of 17.

This is a long and exhaustive process to choose people to stand for a voluntary role! However, it is fundamentally better than asking members of a political party if they'll please, pretty please, stand. It's a measure of IfF's success that we've been able to find more potential candidates than seats available and well-qualified people to carry out the selection role. Using an independent selection panel is also important because it provides a way for those who deeply support the group and its aims but, for whatever reason, don't want to stand, to still play a central role.

Should you use positive discrimination as selection tool?

It is possible to set criteria to ensure the list of candidates includes more women, youth, disabled, right-wing politics or any other factor. According to a BBC survey, the average age of a local councillor is 59, 25% have served for more than 10 years, 60% are men (and probably called David or John), and just 11% are aged under 45. Clearly, there's plenty of space for trying to choose a more representative group. Of course, the carefully balanced team of candidates still has to get elected, but there's still a strong case to be made for ensuring you start with as representative a group as possible.

In both 2015 and 2019 I held discussions to encourage people to stand because they represented a particular group of citizens that would otherwise be missing. In some cases, I regret that, as I let my desire to have a range of people available for selection override more careful consideration of whether they would make good councillors. It is a credit to the selection panels that in both years they were largely able to address the temptation, ultimately selecting competence over labels.

Choosing wards

Who stands where can be a contentious issue. Our baseline has always been that you get the ward you live in. Inevitably, there are too many potential candidates in some places and not enough in others. That means moving some people and with that a greater or lesser likelihood of being elected.

In 2015 the existing councillors made the ward decisions. This had the advantage of using our existing knowledge as councillors; on the other hand, it meant having to work with some people who were unhappy at our decisions. I was selected to stand in a different ward from the one in which I lived. It was a much trickier ward, with two well-established Lib Dems and the leader of the local Tories. This gives some indication of the cockiness of IfF. In the event, we got away with it and I was elected, but I'd have been annoyed had it turned out otherwise.

In 2019 the selection panel made the ward decisions.

In allocating wards, you can look at the probable opposition and estimate the chances your candidate has. Publicly estimating personal strengths also means discussing weaknesses. It means you are placing some people in wards where you anticipate they might lose but are still asking them to put in the same effort. Equally, you may be giving some people an easy ride. All this sets up issues in terms of power and decision making, so I suggest it's best done by the selection group. An alternative is to draw names from a hat; it's a fair method but one that potentially misses opportunities. There is a slightly nerdy additional factor. Where a strong non-independent is judged likely to get in, it can be argued that it's better not to put up more than one independent against them as they will split each other's votes. Of course, the best option, and the one IfF has been lucky enough to have, is to put up a full set of candidates and go for winning everything.

The first meeting of candidates
Over the months between selecting candidates and the election itself, there's potential to create a team who will work together, if elected, to create an ambitious strategy and run an exciting council. The alternative is to take the more traditional route and focus solely on what needs to be done to win seats. There is clearly a balance to be had, and while in 2015 we certainly hoped to win, in 2019 the campaign was called a 'Transition Plan', with the expectation of a new IfF-led council.

That first meeting is when it's often realised that this is indeed a group of disparate individuals with different views and without a common political ideology to cling to. Add to that a mix of existing councillors and new candidates and it makes the use of an experienced external facilitator essential. It's also been helpful to have councillors who aren't standing again available as mentors.

The agenda of the first meeting included exercises to get to know one another and some gentle personal exposure with questions such as:

- Why did you want to do this?
- What things do you need to work at your best?
- What de-motivates and frustrates you?
- What is your hope/fear for your involvement?
- What would we see at the end of your term if we've been successful?

Then time was spent on IfF's common values and our Ways of Working, before signing up people to working groups and allocating key roles, including that of a new IfF convenor to administrate the meetings of the group. IfF has always been keen not to have a 'leader', as this contradicts the ethos of being autonomous individuals.

The first 2015 meeting with candidates included a first go at agreeing priority areas of policy to focus on. Previous experience showed that if asked to focus on the town and not broader issues, most people have more in common than not. By identifying some of those key issues we could then steer the group towards working with them in the campaign.

Part of the feedback from 2015 was that this rush into practical actions and deciding issues we'd campaign on was too early in the process. This was probably because the existing councillors were also central to running the campaign: we were up and off without fully bringing the new people into the group or creating space for new ideas. Learning from this, the first 2019 meeting spent most time on candidates getting to know each other and the team. We focussed on setting out how the campaign would be run, and introduced Slack as our online forum. We also discussed social media and talked about raising funds for the campaign. The meeting set out to make the candidates feel confident the campaign team knew what they were doing – and to provide a taster of what lay ahead.

RUNNING THE CAMPAIGN
Timetables
All three IfF elections have been run on a fairly similar timetable. This meant a series of informal gatherings to entice and inform potential candidates from mid-November to Christmas, followed by applications by the end of January, selection in early February and a first meeting of candidates in mid-February. Assuming elections in the first week of May, this has worked well for us. It's a balance of leaving enough time for the campaign to take effect versus boredom, loss of energy and interest from both candidates and the public that can set in over a longer campaign.

Personnel

In 2015 we had six councillors standing again, many of whom had held key roles in the council and were prepared to take central roles in the campaign. We then recruited a number of key people to help, crucially a campaign manager and a designer. The manager kept things on track (having defined the timetable) and linked all the various parts together. Her role was crucial. The designer was responsible for the visual content of the campaign, leaflets, posters, adverts and so on.

In 2019 that wasn't the case. Only three of those standing again had a full term of experience and none of running a campaign. In addition, we failed to find a volunteer campaign manager, though we did recruit a designer. Fortunately, two of the selection panel, along with a 2011 councillor and someone with extensive media skills, stepped in to effectively run the campaign.

While it was clear that the campaign belonged to the candidates, in the initial stages especially, this external group took the lead.

The campaign team brought in some existing councillors for support in specific areas, and I attended a few meetings to provide some thoughts. To me it felt important to be available but, as I was not standing again, also to be clearly fading away. I believe the candidates needed to own the campaign for many reasons, primarily because if elected, they'd be on their own as councillors. A key challenge for the campaign team was to ensure they did not take on more ownership and responsibility than was necessary.

There is a case to be made that the decision to run the 2019 campaign as preparation for power led to excessive input by the campaign team. Their weekly meetings included detailed inputs on areas such as the future of local government and current Frome Council strategy. It would have been perfectly possible to run, and win, the campaign without this. On the downside, the candidates took longer to make the campaign their own; on the upside, as councillors they are remarkably well prepared now to start creating their own informed strategy.

There is a copy (with names changed) of the 'IfF timetable towards success' in the resources section of the Flatpack Democracy website.

The volunteers who come forward to run and support a campaign will obviously bring their own strengths, weaknesses and agendas. IfF and Frome have been extraordinarily blessed with the quality of this wider group who support the councillors.

Costs and fundraising

In 2015, an initial £25 from each candidate gave a solid working sum of £425. From this we spent £125 on a professional crowdfunding platform and gave ourselves a few weeks to raise £2,000. In the event, we raised this within a few days, and we ran the campaign for slightly under £2,700. This is around £160 per candidate (way below the allowance of £740, plus 6p per elector).

Having a decent budget led to paying for new materials for boards to go outside of houses and stickers for the artwork (rather than paper and glue). Printing of each of the three leaflets was between £200 and £300 (for 11,000 copies). Other expenses included a leaflet translated into Polish to reach this significant group in Frome, who might well otherwise have not taken part; badges; a banner; and the 'I'm for Frome' video, which cost a bargain £600.

Without the video, the 2019 campaign cost just under £1,500 (£90 per candidate), with £1,000 of that spent on three leaflets.

The 2019 crowdfunder took much longer, making its £1,500 target in 35 days with a surprisingly small 53 donors. (Other towns also struggled with crowdfunding, and it may be that it has become a less attractive way to raise funds.)

The fundraising and associated social media has the additional benefit of enabling a wider group to get involved in a positive way. It also enables candidates already putting in hours not to have to pay for campaign materials as well, so in that way it doesn't deter those with less income.

Overall we recognised that a key challenge would be introducing, or reintroducing, IfF. Frome's population has continued to grow dramatically over the past few years and the majority of inhabitants are probably only vaguely aware there is a town council, let alone what it does.

Strategy

In every IfF campaign we've held regular meetings for all candidates and a collection of group meetings to take on key issues. I'll only focus on aspects that are significant additions and changes from the 2011 campaign described in *Flatpack Democracy.*

Both campaigns took time to support candidates in marketing themselves with excellent descriptions and photographs. In 2019, three timed phases were clearly set out:

1) Building the group and collecting their ideas.
2) A soft campaign that would build public profile and start to raise issues.
3) The campaign proper, with leaflets and social media, etc.

These overlapped, covering mid-February to the May elections and the weekly meetings then linked to these broad areas. Layered onto these phases were the key areas that needed to be agreed and communicated in each of the three leaflets.

The principles behind our communication strategy

At the start of the 2015 campaign some principles were set out by Mel Usher based on previous experiences; these remained essentially the same in 2019.

1) Our campaign will remain positive. We'll focus on what IfF is, what it has already achieved, who we are now and what we want to achieve in the next four years. We will avoid mentioning opponents or other local authorities.

2) We'll run a different type of campaign. We can't compete against the big political parties by doing what they do. They do it better than we ever will. We'll instead build a campaign around direct action and unusual and wacky events.

3) Branding will remain consistent and obvious. Our key and most recognisable acronym is IfF. We must continue to use it but in new and interesting ways like: I'm For Frome, the Big IFF, Independent Fabulous Frome, Ideas for Frome etc. There will be a standard look and feel to all materials produced (in the end we focussed on I'm for Frome).

4) We'll rely on support from others. We'll make use of supporters and gather more wherever possible.

5) We'll always be clear about IfF as a concept. We aren't a political party in the traditional sense, and thus not bound by ideology or party whip. IfF exists solely to support good people, who wouldn't otherwise stand, to become elected representatives.

6) We'll stress that it's our ambition that sets IfF apart and provides a real choice for Frome.

What we set out to communicate

What makes the IfF model significantly different is that there's no manifesto. There isn't a promised set of policies or strategy. Instead there are the core values and a commitment to engage.

While in 2011 IfF had largely campaigned on an offer of change: anything will be better than what we have. It was clear that in 2015 there had to be some reference to what had been achieved and some broad areas that would be addressed. By 2019 this had changed even further to focus clearly on what IfF had done so far before introducing new areas for attention.

This link to the past is slightly spurious, but it makes sense in terms of being re-elected. There is no guarantee that the new group will behave in any of the same ways as the previous council, nor does one group's achievement necessarily lead to those of another. However, I'd argue this is increasingly true of political parties, who campaign on a manifesto that is often forgotten, ignored or changed.

We arrived at the 2015 IfF approach by facilitated discussion. This lead to an agreement to campaign under four main headings:
1) **Wellbeing.** This category includes sport, community groups, arts and culture, dog walking, intergenerational projects, dog shit and the new Frome Town Hall.
2) **Active democracy.** This focuses on inclusion, better communications within Frome, more participation and civic pride (primarily street cleanliness).
3) **Poverty.** This addresses employment, apprenticeships, youth training, green jobs, the car club, Fair Frome, education and joined up transport.
4) **Appropriate development.** This covers the areas we can control, like the river corridor and green spaces, and areas we can lobby for, like the development of a large brownfield site in the town centre for jobs and shops.

This covered a range of policy and projects, some 'how' and some 'what'. There was nothing hugely contentious and the range allowed different candidates to focus on their own area of expertise and interest.

As mentioned earlier, the 2019 group were much more overtly prepared for power. They'd spent considerable facilitated time homing in on issues they intended to focus on once elected. These issues were then reflected in communications to the electorate. So, this is a balance, depending on whether the independents are new or established, as well as a calculated guess as to whether the group will end up running the council.

The electoral challenge of community building

IfF's approach of empowering the community has a fundamental flaw when it comes to election time. It's our principle not to claim ideas or project successes so that the community group that carries out the project gets maximum profile. This builds their confidence and reinforces the intent to reposition the council as a facilitating and supporting body. At election time, however, this leaves IfF without the positive publicity of being able to show their involvement in successful community projects. Instead, we use news stories to build up IfF's profile as quickly as possible without sinking to the level of suddenly claiming everything good that's happened in the town.

Focussing on IfF as the local choice is a powerful message. The district council is so disliked we could have got elected just by not being them, but that's hard to do while being positive. We did, however, clearly separate ourselves from them, stressing that money raised by Frome's council is only spent in Frome.

As our campaign went out of its way to point out: '*We are the ONLY local candidates to vote for at a town level; you may have voted for your party for the district or MP, but it's now time to put party politics aside and think of FROME; it's worth voting for us on our past TRACK RECORD and future plans; something GOOD is happening here for the town but only because of IfF being INDEPENDENT.*"

The tricky issue of communicating in multi-seat wards

Where there's more than one seat per ward (and more than one vote to cast) there's a challenge in guiding people on how to vote. Ideally, we'd like them to use all their votes for the independents, and we went to considerable lengths to try and explain this. It's most important they don't use one vote for the independent they know, and then either use their other votes for non-independents or waste them.

Wacky ideas

Another of those tricky balances is to put forward serious ideas and proposals alongside upbeat, different and sometimes pretty wacky ideas. A commitment to this principle is, however, at the core of what IfF is. I am delighted about this, mainly because there have been many moments in the last eight years that have been seriously good fun. I don't believe I could possibly have stayed engaged for this long without that commitment. For me an IfF campaign has to err on the side of extreme silliness and take some risks.

Millie supports #independentsfurfrome

In 2015 we had a 'flash mob' at the train station to sing the weary workers home to the place they loved with the song 'Welcome Home'. Amongst our candidates was local musician Al O'Kane. The creative combination of Al's musicianship and Howard Vause led to a video highlighting a number of key ideas: 'Typical Frome, always doing their own thing... 'for the people, by the people... and of course 'I'm For Frome'. It also contains a version of Bob Dylan's 'Don't Look Back' single word messages, in this case a list of all IfF's achievements to date.

The video did many things. It was fantastically bonding for us as a group as all the councillors took part in the filming; it targeted groups, especially young voters, we probably failed to reach in other ways; and it gave Al some great exposure. As a councillor, he went on to focus on work with the arts. In addition the video provided a tangible campaign focus, especially for the many supporters who contributed to the crowdfunding. Did it bring in many new votes? We don't know. While it cost a significant portion of our campaign funds, this didn't present us with a problem. My conclusion is that significant one-off 'wacky events' like this are well worth creating primarily because they create the message that we're different.

The 2019 campaign had some different 'wacky' elements: a #independentsfurfrome event, which involved using lots of dogs in rosettes to spread the message. Four candidates and supporters ran between the polling stations on polling day, and this was well covered on social media. There was also an 'IfF only' Facebook hustings, where three candidates answered people's questions. For the online hustings we had some pre-prepared questions and answers, but what was great was that the conversation could go on after the hour. This provided an opportunity to go into detail about our principles and ideas, and the video was then available for anyone to view afterwards.

Traditional campaigning

Despite the hype about difference, IfF has always done the traditional thing of leaflets through letterboxes, and posters and notices on boards in gardens. We've combined leaflets and posters so that the leaflet can be read, then stuck in a window. We've kept messaging as simple as possible. We've used a great professional designer, and what a difference that makes!

It's tempting to think the majority of leaflets hit the recycling before they're read. While this may be true, as it's mostly older people who vote and still have faith in the electoral process, they're the ones most likely to have the time to read what's on offer. And as mentioned endlessly, results are often decided on very few votes. I kept in mind that the leaflet that trapped my fingers in the letterbox when out delivering on a wet Wednesday could be the one that decides the election.

Leaflets

In both campaigns we had three leaflets. The nature of the content was broadly the same (and is summarised below). However, for the really keen, the 2019 leaflets can be found in the resources section of the *Flatpack Democracy* website.

The first leaflet, generally delivered in late March, was to bring people up to speed with what had been done so far. The second introduced the candidates for that ward and let people know they could vote for all three candidates (we aimed to deliver this before postal voting started). The third leaflet, delivered just before the election, was a simple A5 reminder of the election and, of course, an exhortation to vote IfF.

In both campaigns candidates were encouraged to work together to leaflet their areas and build their own team of volunteers. Towards the end there was some wider support where groups hit areas especially tiresome to leaflet. While all this can seem terribly tedious at times, with the promise of a pint in the pub after, it's another thing that can bring a group together.

Social media and website

Since 2011, the whole world of social media has grown. These days, it's easy to make and share short films and candidate profiles; we did this, always making sure we linked back to the website. The website allowed some longer, more in-depth pieces to be written and became the home for our FAQs and a series of short films. Both campaigns spent time preparing the candidates to answer anticipated tricky questions. Yet again, we were massively helped by excellent filmmakers delighted to be involved in something they believed in, as long as it didn't impact excessively on their work. By the 2019 campaign, these short films and graphics were a major feature of our communications outside of our leaflets.

In social media, as with all other forms of communication, we followed the same IfF rules: relentless positivity and not engaging with the general trolling and annoying nonsense, like irrelevant comments, that social media can sometimes throw up.

The town council and the elections

Council staff must, of course, retain careful impartiality at all times. Councillors are also not allowed to use their official role to campaign in what's called a period of 'purdah'. This is usually for six weeks before the election. This doesn't stop a councillor from campaigning, but would, for example, stop the mayor from talking about IfF's achievements rather than those of the council.

In 2015, the council did, however, run 'Democracy Day' in association with a collection of church groups. This was primarily the hustings event for the general election but included a broader opportunity for candidates at all levels to be present and informally questioned. Local radio covered the event.

The results

In pre-IfF days up to half of the seats in Frome were 'co-opted' because the parties could not find enough candidates. That changed with IfF. In 2011 there were 43 candidates and 13,000 more votes cast, and in 2015 that rose to 49 candidates, with 6,000 additional votes. In 2019, without a simultaneous general election and with the collapse of party opposition, the votes cast fell by 12,000 and the number of candidates was down to 36.

The count

Four months after seeking candidates, the whole election campaign comes to its peak in an agricultural show cattle shed near Frome. For anyone who hasn't been to an electoral count, it's good theatre. Tables are set out with piles of papers that you can peer at and compare the heights of. Where there are multiple candidates in single wards, it gets horribly complicated. Eventually, the presiding officer takes group leaders to one side and sees if they're happy with what is about to be announced, at which point someone can demand a recount if the result is close. Then the results are declared.

In the 2015 elections IfF candidates won, often by large majorities, though not always. Al O'Kane won by 17 votes in 2015 in the same ward as myself, where the local Tory leader was denied a third recount. In 2019 IfF took nearly 80% of the total vote. The tension was greatest in 2015 when we reached the last seat to be declared: would Sheila Gore be the 1/17 not elected? Luckily she won, creating an extraordinarily unlikely 17/17, all to be repeated in 2019 with Sheila last again.

Of course by the time of the count we were existing in a tiny bubble awash with adrenalin, with the few people who really cared about the results together in one room. In 2015 I had honestly expected the parties to focus on the district and national elections and leave Frome to IfF, given the job we'd done already. The fact that they put so much effort in trying to win back the town only illustrates again the confrontational nature of our system. Satisfyingly, the 2015 landslide proved significantly newsworthy to result in a long *Guardian* article and a real feeling of achievement throughout the town.

Triumphalism

The other side of our IfF victories were, of course, defeats for others who also cared about Frome. In 2011, some of our party opposition had indulged in very personal attacks and there was, unsurprisingly, some pleasure in their defeat. By 2015, we'd got better at restraining any overt triumphalism. I do know, though, that some of those who were not elected felt deeply hurt. I'd underestimated how much being on the council meant to them. Their status, power and ego took a big knock as well as their social life. Interestingly, while some of the IfF group are personal friends, it's never become a group in that way. Perhaps the independent selection process helps with this, with candidates being drawn from the wider community rather than members of a small club.

Ultimately, we live in the same community. It's especially unhelpful to start a council with personal issues and animosities between councillors unresolved. The 2011 council effectively lost seven of its members (the non IfF councillors) and they never really contributed again after losing overall power. In 2015 the issue was different, but those defeated have other roles in the community, including many who are elected at other levels of government. The IfF Ways of Working might have guided us towards handling their defeat better.

In general, though, IfF has tended to work through these issues and get on with the business of running Frome. I can see this would be more difficult where victory has been by a slim majority. We've heard from other independents that this can be especially problematic where the town clerk and other staff retain a close relationship with the remaining old guard and/or are resistant to change.

Keeping in touch

IfF hasn't done well at keeping people on board who weren't selected as candidates or those who weren't elected in 2011. These are people who've taken the huge step of putting themselves up for election and invested considerable time in the process; losing while others go on to become councillors and even run the council may not be easy for them. I have three comments on this issue.

Firstly, there may be other roles within the town where they can be steered to use the skills and energy they offered. In 2011, some of those not elected quickly found positions in key local charities.

Secondly, there is the issue of retaining support for IfF. We've not been good at keeping links with those not initially selected, those not elected or those who've played key support roles in the campaigns. Simply ensuring these people are properly acknowledged may be enough, though it also raises the question of whether IfF has 'friends' or even 'members'. How then to stop the slippery slope to IfF emerging as a 'local party'?

Thirdly, there's an issue that might belong to the council as well as IfF: is there any advantage in keeping ex-councillors in the loop? This was traditionally the role of aldermen, who since 1974 have had no voting rights. They could be elected by new councillors from those leaving in order to retain their services for the benefit of the area. District councils (but not town) can still confer the honorary title of alderman or alderwomen on persons who have 'rendered eminent services'.

My experience of leaving other significant roles is that as soon as my coat is off the peg I'm quickly forgotten. In many ways that seems right, certainly in terms of ensuring the new incumbents make the role their own. It does, however, mean some useful experience can walk away too.

The analysis

Group or Party	2011 votes	2011 %	2015 votes	2015 %	2019 votes	2019 %
IfF	9452	45%	14,542	54%	12,578	79%
Con	5377	26%	4,731	17%	684	4%
LD	4712	22%	5,158	19%	0	0
Lab	1018	5%	974	4%	1947	12%
UKIP			1,763	7%	0	0
Other			663	4%		
Total Votes	21,007		27,168		15,842	

I've consistently lambasted the UK's first-past-the-post system, regularly declaring democracy to be a farce. Roughly two thirds of registered voters voted in 2015, little more than half that in 2019. In both cases, a proportional voting system would still have given IfF an outright majority. In 2015 it would've come down to a majority of one, and in 2019 Labour would've gained two seats, with IfF holding the rest.

Fellow Councillor Toby Eliot's take was this: *"I've been concerned that we (as an electorate) have confused our democracy with our political parties, that we think having a say means making a choice between what's on offer nationally. For me that's what IfF is about – reclaiming our democracy from the national political parties. However, the voters of Frome clearly aren't confused about democracy and political parties and, given another choice, have been able to discern the advantage of ambition for the town over ambition for a party or ideology."*

I agree, and it's also true that analysing the results of the elections along traditional lines fails to recognise the different paradigm that is IfF: it is all parties and none. If the right people can be persuaded to come forward and the selection process works, then a full IfF council will contain a significant cross-section of views. Where some are missing, they will be picked up through careful participative actions in the wider community. This is the exact opposite to the triumphal winner takes all system we currently operate in the UK.

Why did IfF win so conclusively in 2015?

I've used Mel Usher's analysis (allegedly written the day after the count whilst under the influence of a massive hangover). It covers both the campaign and key elements that created the foundations for IfF support.

- **A Plan.** We had one (well, sort of). This was about the future of the town and called 'A Strategy for Success'. This was based on the Vision for Frome's Community Plan, which was probably the biggest consultation exercise undertaken in Frome's history, but until IfF came along had no means of being implemented. We also had an implied plan that was to spend the first three and a half years rebuilding the reputation of the town council, not IfF. That meant we didn't have to get involved in dogfights with traditional politicians.
- **Inclusivity.** We've been very open, welcoming and transparent in meetings and online. Gone is the old stuffiness and 'we know best' attitude.
- **Positivity.** Apart from our potshots at the district, we've stayed relentlessly upbeat about Frome and its people. This attitude has paid off in local, regional, national and international media; if we also attract more investment, visitors and engaged people, that's a bonus.
- **Engagement.** We've been patchy on engagement but are still far better than most other councils, especially at this level. We've formed some great alliances with other groups and bodies in the town and this has been a major strength. There was a light bulb moment a couple of years ago that centred around this realisation: 'if we don't let people know what we're up to, how can they be engaged?'
- **Staff.** We've been good at enticing, employing and trusting the staff to get on with their jobs. Budgeting, whether on revenue or capital, has been excellent.
- **Projects.** Our emphasis on big projects has meant we're the only public body seen to be investing in the town; indeed, the district and county are withdrawing. We've been incredibly flexible in our approach: if it's looked good and we've had the money, we've taken the project forward.
- **Progressive localism.** A tricky concept but one that thankfully is not defined by left or right wing labels. In times of uncertainty and rapid change people want to feel they can get involved and influence events. Have we finally got our message across about the problems with parties at local level? Maybe so, although how we handle no opposition will be crucial too.
- **Councillors.** Traditional politicians said we wouldn't last until Christmas. We've held together remarkably well, and most of us have been able to contribute in areas we've been interested in and to the degree which we felt able. The work was not divided up formally; individuals picked up projects and ran with them. This was a bit random but worked well; it may, however, be too loose now that we have 17 councillors. It's fair to say the opposition councillors made very little contribution. This had the knock-on effect that we were sorely underrepresented in the district, who were used to dealing with town councils through district councillors.

- **The Election**. Clearly IfF picks up extra votes, and a greater proportion, by being able to field a full set of candidates. The plan was that in the polling booth voters thought first of IfF when it came to local matters. The 'I'm For Frome' logo subtly cast the other candidates as 'Not for Frome' – unfair but smart. We looked like a cohesive team, whereas the others were a raggedy bunch of individuals.
- **Social Media**. This allowed us to be playful and fun and again, and we won hands-down on that score. Politics can be serious but doesn't need to be solemn.
- **Leaflets and Boards.** Clear and precise, no flashy, coloured brochures and a whole town coverage at nicely-timed intervals: the strategy worked.
- **Timing and candidate selection.** The timing was pretty spot-on, and candidate selection worked well.
- **Money**. The crowdfunding was essential to run a decent campaign
- **End result?** Wipe out.

Two further comments on the results are interesting. Charles Wood, long time local Tory leader and a man who always understood the IfF approach, while retaining the role of firm opposition, wrote this for the local Tory Party: *"A really big limitation on getting good, initiating, and active councillors is the small pool represented by the party 'got to be a member' criteria. So a few stand time and again, and even fewer get elected time and again. This lack of fresh blood, of new ideas, of new energy, and sometimes of competent balanced views and decision making ability, was the cause of the downfall in favour of an IfF that could recruit from every corner of the Frome community. This remains a huge challenge for us members of a party that still wish to stand for election under its banner and with a particular view on what is good for Frome, which will not always, or even often, necessarily be different in outcome to that of the IfF, albeit the means of getting there may differ.'*

The view of a senior local Lib Dem was this: *"I would agree with the Greens that it's madness to compete. I will encourage party members to apply to IfF selection if they can agree with your Ways of Working (as members of another party do). I know many town councils and smaller parish councils have depoliticised elections, so why not Frome, I don't know. People need a choice between candidates but you've effectively defeated party politics in Frome town council twice now."*

Final comments on the 2019 election

The 2019 Putinesque victory with 79.4% of the votes owes itself to three main factors:
1) A significant majority of the voters of Frome who made the effort to vote recognised the huge benefits the first two IfF councils brought to Frome, and they want more of the same

2) Over a third of votes in 2015 were for the Lib Dems or Tories. The former withdrew to focus on the district, where they won control, and the latter collapsed. Labour have been traditionally weak in Frome and ran a poor, cantankerous, uninspiring campaign. Thus we enjoyed a lack of opposition critical to our success

3) Deep disillusionment with the political parties due to their failure to enact Brexit: although irrelevant at town level, it's likely this turned some voters away from the parties and towards independents like IfF.

What next?

Two key questions are left hanging from this chapter: Firstly, can any of this be replicated elsewhere? We'll come to this in Chapter 8. Secondly, does the selection group effectively choose the next council? While I've set out above why a totally IfF council does not represent a dictatorship, there's an issue to confront around how candidates are selected. In both the last two elections, the IfF selection group effectively chose the council. This was especially true in 2019, where the best a party candidate could do was to gain only half the votes of her nearest IfF rival.

Perhaps ideally, there would be 'primaries' to select the IfF candidates. So the selection group mentioned earlier is replaced by a panel made up of a cross-section of residents and businesses. What form this panel might take would be a challenge. How do we ensure the loudest man or most charismatic candidate doesn't automatically come out on top? There's a risk too that through a competitive selection process, divisions would be highlighted as a starting point rather than focussing on common ground. And would there ever be the energy and enthusiasm to arrange all this for what is, after all, just a parish election?

It may also be that the selection process we've come up with leads to a group of skilled, enthusiastic and experienced people being able to take a position in the community that lets them genuinely contribute.

4. What IfF did

MAKE YOUR MARK
REGISTER TO VOTE
www.gov.uk/register-to-vote [X]

I'M FOR FROME

KEEP FROME TOWN COUNCIL INDEPENDENT

VOTE IFF ON 7TH MAY

ifF
INDEPENDENTS
FOR FROME

IfF is a group of local people who care about our community and want to do the best for Frome. We came together in 2011 when Frome voted for an IfF-led town council.

Spot the DIFFerence four years have made...

Sustainable funding for positive change - The Cheese and Grain has a new look and new facilities. It is now self-financing and more popular than ever.

Investing in and protecting our open spaces - The Showfield is safe from further development, the Dippy and Whatcombe Fields belong to Frome.

Supporting local people – We have funded and helped to obtain funding for more than 90 local organisations, including Fair Frome. Because of IfF's help, Frome has nearly 100 new allotments.

Education, training and play – amongst others we've supported the Welshmill pump track, the Children's Festival, Edventure, Mindset, new equipment and the games area in Mary Bailey Playing Field and the Roller Disco.

Clean and green – Our electric car club is cheaper and greener than owning a car. We won a major Green Energy award in 2014 and solar panels are reducing energy use AND earning money for Frome.

We have secured local assets through careful planning, brought in over £1.9m for community projects, balanced the books and increased Frome's cash reserve.

These are just some of our proudest achievements and we've lots more big ideas for our small town. Vote IfF on 7th May and keep our council open, active and independent.

www.iffrome.org.uk   ifF
INDEPENDENTS
FOR FROME

Introduction

This chapter covers how Independents for Frome has moved on from its 2011 incarnation. It focuses on IfF's structure and internal changes. With all the councillors being from IfF, it can be tricky to separate what IfF has done and what the council has achieved. Clearly, the two are inextricably linked, but Chapter 5 focuses on what's been achieved for the town by the council.

Of course, we were delighted in 2015 to win all 17 seats. But all belonging to the same group brings its own challenges. IfF does have a range of views and ideologies within the group, never mind the range of personalities, experiences and skills, but I'd underestimated the way that a formal opposition, however ineffective, was useful in bringing us together.

This 2015 group, however large, also faced the problem of not being the initial revolutionaries: the energy of consolidation is very different to that of creation. In addition, there were seven people with previous councillor experience. This clearly had considerable influence over shaping the direction of the incoming council, if only because they knew how it all worked.

Introduction

This chapter covers how Independents for Frome has moved on from its 2011 incarnation. It focuses on IfF's structure and internal changes. With all the councillors being from IfF, it can be tricky to separate what IfF has done and what the council has achieved. Clearly, the two are inextricably linked, but Chapter 5 focuses on what's been achieved for the town by the council.

Of course, we were delighted in 2015 to win all 17 seats. But all belonging to the same group brings its own challenges. IfF does have a range of views and ideologies within the group, never mind the range of personalities, experiences and skills, but I'd underestimated the way that a formal opposition, however ineffective, was useful in bringing us together.

This 2015 group, however large, also faced the problem of not being the initial revolutionaries: the energy of consolidation is very different to that of creation. In addition, there were seven people with previous councillor experience. This clearly had considerable influence over shaping the direction of the incoming council, if only because they knew how it all worked.

The town council strategy

Because all councillors are from the IfF group, one could argue that the council strategy is also an IfF strategy. Alongside the three pillars of wellbeing, prosperity and environmental sustainability that support everything we do, there are five things we keep in mind when putting our policies into practice.
- Be bold
- Encourage involvement
- Enable others to succeed
- Campaign, lobby and lead
- Practice what we preach

Perhaps this is as close as we ever come to an IfF ethos.

Do all these fine words affect the projects the council has carried out?

Below are three examples of how council actions have been shaped by the IfF ethos.
1) We've changed the relationship between the town and the council by doing things 'with' the community, not 'to' it. For example, we purchased new allotments and then handed full control and funding to the Allotment Association. We created panels where townspeople could come together in large

numbers to address specific issues and take direct actions. We also created the Peoples' Budget, which lets the community allocate significant sums to projects of their choosing.

2) We've enabled members of the community to bring their ideas to the council, who then, where required, have provided resources and support. This is central to our aim of building the profile of those who are active in the wider community but aren't members of the council or IfF. The best example of this is Fair Frome. It was set up via the council but is now an independent charity campaigning around poverty and running the foodbank and furniture recycling project. Overall, there are ten community groups we've given the stability of on-going grants and access to additional guidance and support should they need it.

3) Because we haven't been afraid to try new things, we've achieved much more than previous Frome councils. For example, the renovation of The Cheese and Grain, which is now a community hall, regional venue and training hub, was an ambitious project and entailed a degree of risk. Another project has been ensuring the community of Frome has a say in the development of Saxonvale. Saxonvale is a 12-acre former industrial site in the centre of Frome that's been derelict for decades. The town council bought a portion of the land and then pushed successfully to persuade the other landholders to combine and sell their land for development. Finally, we've not been afraid to try new ideas, like a Frome crowdfunding platform; in the end, our crowdfunding didn't work, but the point is that we've never been afraid to experiment.

What, no manifesto?

When IfF first stood for election, the situation was sufficiently dire for people to risk voting for change, partly because whatever happened could hardly be worse. The second time around, in 2015, it was slightly more tricky. While IfF had clearly achieved a great deal, we were now putting forward a new group of councillors who could, in theory, do things of less benefit to the community.

The easiest way out of this predicament would've been to publish a public manifesto of IfF's intentions, motives and views. But how could we create a manifesto while still allowing elected councillors to have their own, authentic views and truly be independents? Our approach was to be deliberately unspecific in our election materials (leaflets, brochures etc.) about what we were going to do. Instead, we talked about our commitment to finishing every project we started; to wellbeing, sports and the arts; to housing, employment and health; and to addressing inequality. I found this slightly uncomfortable as our approach started to resemble that of the other political parties. However, we were committed to allowing the public to have a key role in deciding what they wanted to happen. Our election material also talked about listening, engaging and communicating more, a crucial and recurring theme that puts how IfF works at the centre of what we're offering.

Do the 'essentials' I set out in 2014 still hold?

In *Flatpack Democracy* I set out what I considered the five 'essentials' to getting elected. I'll first outline and briefly comment on these, and then I'll look at some specific challenges relating to them. (In Chapter 8 I'll look at them again in relation to how other groups have changed and used them.)

1) **Work as a group.** When I wrote this in 2014, it applied to getting elected; it still applies. What's more, once elected if you're to really make a difference, or to be an effective opposition, I believe independents still need to work well together.

2) **Agree your Ways of Working.** I still maintain that a set of values is essential to keep your eyes on the prize. Disagreement and diversity are to be encouraged, but the confrontation that besets British politics is a disaster. Without some form of agreed Ways of Working, a group of voluntary councillors will never achieve what's increasingly required of them.

3) **Use a facilitator.** This is vital at the inception of any group, and we've used facilitation at key moments throughout IfF's life. As individuals, we picked up facilitation skills as we went along, so the need to bring in outside help has been reduced.

4) **Get all the help you can.** This applied initially to getting elected; later, it morphed into a key element of IfF's strategy. The council and councillors should only be one aspect of a joined-up community. The IfF-led councils made this the core of their strategy to great effect.

5) **Keep it light.** The second IfF group has done well in retaining a lightness and capacity for wit. This has largely taken us through the inevitable boring bits with our values and 'essentials' interact. Being prepared to listen and compromise enabled that lightness of touch; a question we often ask ourselves is this: do you want to be happy or do you want to be right?

Three further comments on the essentials

Firstly, the aspect of 'work as a group', which I think we managed well, was to build and maintain trust in each other's decision making. There are many reasons for this, but the most important is that any individual councillor won't be able to engage with absolutely everything; in some areas, others will do the work and make the decisions. And if you weren't involved in the process, you must accept the decision. There are few things more time consuming, annoying and undermining than councillors emerging from outside the decision-making process to question the work of others. Rear Admiral Grace Murray Hopper is credited with having said: "*Better to seek forgiveness than to ask permission.*" The idea that we should build and maintain a working practice that encourages risk and creative thinking could be seen as more of an important aspiration than an additional essential. However, without this ambition it is hard to see how a council can become truly effective. Of course, it's public money we're dealing with and health and safety is paramount, but frankly you don't get remembered or re-elected for being safe and sound. My view is that unless ambition and risk can become part of the package, many of the other actions I mention will not happen.

Thirdly, I commented above that many of the IfF councillors have, in effect, become facilitators, especially our mayors and chairs. Defining facilitation as making easy 'the act of assisting' or 'the progress or improvement of something'. It's crucial not to take this skill for granted. Perhaps IfF has been lucky in our choices of facilitators, but it's also been a process of learning from each other and the facilitators we have brought in. Of course a good traditional chair will regulate the flow of discussion, drawing out quiet people or those with the most relevant expertise and limiting those who tend to do a lot of the talking. But so often the mayors and chairs I have seen elsewhere are nowhere near achieving this. So much of what IfF has set out to achieve, both internally and in our relationship to Frome, definitely couldn't have been achieved without the use of solid facilitation methods by councillors and staff.

SO HAVE THE LAST FIVE YEARS ALL BEEN PERFECT?
How the group worked together and some early challenges
Following a very busy 2015 as mayor and the election campaign, I went on holiday almost immediately after the new council was formally ensconced. I was, however, there for an initial meeting, where we proposed the first mayor of the new council and various other roles were assigned.

My view of that meeting is that we jumped far too quickly into product over process. We misunderstood the difference between working as a campaign group with a clear goal and the need to create a cohesive group of councillors, most of whom were starting out from different places. This initiated a number of misunderstandings that took a long time to recover from and also reduced the potential input from the ten new councillors.

This wasn't a disaster, but it set in place a 'this is how we work' pattern, which was hard for new people to challenge. To compound this, the original plan for a party conference, at which we'd go off for a few days together, was delayed until the autumn, missing an early opportunity to get back on track.

A key first task of the 2015 council was to create a new strategy for the next four years. The (self selected) group who led on this were largely new councillors, who set out their own way to complete the task. This again highlighted the dilemma of process vs product very starkly. It also seriously tested the intent IfF has to trust and have confidence and optimism in other people's expertise, knowledge and intentions. Without the early work of getting to know each other better and without any IfF strategy on how to deal with conflict, considerable damage was done that I feel reduced the group's potential later.

That lack of thinking around conflict resolution and the allied question of how to give constructive feedback is a crucial area that needs looking at to reduce the risk of leaderless groups imploding.

Of course, it's easy to make these judgements in hindsight. We were all keen to get on with things and there was a need to put in place a structure that the staff could work with. The alternative view is that 'you can't make an omelette without breaking eggs'. I'd say that it's very hard to stick to the IfF Ways of Working if too much omelette making is going on. And as many of the new councillors joined because of the IfF values, it was confusing for them to see this happening.

How successful has IfF been in keeping councillors engaged over time?

The system IfF uses to encourage and select councillors has, in the main, been highly successful. IfF councillors have been local people of significant experience and skills, who would never have come to these council roles under the traditional routes of party selection. Inevitably, some have had more time and/or ways to engage than others. But five years in, the vast majority of councillors continue to attend every committee they are on (and many they don't have to) and to play full roles in other events.

We did effectively lose three councillors on the way. One councillor struggled consistently with the challenges of single parenthood and a lack of resources. Even though the council provided a range of support in terms of childcare and remote working, we could probably have done more to ensure her engagement. A second councillor never really seemed to take on board the way that an IfF council is different from other councils: he wanted to work more as an individual than a member of the group, so he struggled to fit in, and we struggled to deal with this. In his case, we should have referred to our Ways of Working in order to move forward positively. The third leaver underestimated her own workload, and our efforts to help keep her on board couldn't help.

In the first 2011 IfF council, we started with ten active councillors and finished with perhaps six well engaged. More so-called normal councils, with a set of councillors in opposition, will often end up with very few actively engaged. With 17 councillors in 2015, losing three did not have a major impact; however, we did miss the unique experiences and expertise these councillors could have brought to the table.

In only one of these cases did the person leave Frome, forcing a by-election which IfF won with over half the votes. It was right to have provided the opportunity for choice, though at a cost of £6,000 and with just over a year to run before the 2019 election, it was also slightly annoying!

More disappointingly, in my view, we've failed to use the Ways of Working to get the most from our councillors. The group has developed cliques who share greater trust and others are left out. Rereading the ways we set out to challenge ourselves to adhere to the core values, they make a great list. While they underpinned how IfF has operated to a large degree, we've not created the opportunities or relationships to really push each other on these values.

We also shouldn't have expected new councillors to know what they needed to know or to feel unable to ask for help. One of the potential key roles of the new councillors is to question everything, keeping the old ones on their toes.

However it all basically functions pretty well. The IfF approach is evolving and can be taken up by others in Frome and elsewhere, they could build on the experiment and find ways to extract more for the common good.

Working with the staff and council systems

Similarly we made assumptions in relation to the staff. A quick introduction at a council meeting does not set up the start of a working relationship, and we should've had a facilitated workshop soon after the election. We probably got lost in the logistics of arranging large meetings and ended up postponing events because too many people couldn't come.

New councillors will often come in with a mass of new ideas. To quickly build a relationship where staff can both hear these ideas but also share their experiences and feel able to challenge them is essential. The IfF councils have had significantly different relationships between staff and councillors than most councils, and there's been a real sense of mutual respect.

The mix of new and seasoned councillors was probably behind a lack of sufficient briefing on the council year with its budget cycles and timings, because we assumed that everyone knew what was going to happen and when. One good idea put forward was for each council employee to make a short film about themselves and their work so the councillors could better understand their role.

The problems with the system... and the clerk

My eight years' experience as a town councillor has led me to face the reality that the current democratic system at town and parish council level is structurally flawed. Although there are many ways to run organisations, few are designed with the inbuilt dysfunctionality of a council.

It starts with the fact that every four years a new set of managers is brought in. Some may have worked in the organisation before, but not necessarily. At a town or parish level, all these people are volunteers. They bring with them a range of skills and experiences which may or may not be relevant or useful. While overall they're a group that sets out to work together to make sound decisions, they're often divided into subgroups that oppose each other. They elect a chairperson, who is not really a leader and to whom only their own group is likely to be loyal.

These managers are supposed to control the strategy and work of the organisation. However, there is another manager – the paid town clerk. This person may have held the job for many years. They manage the staff and have very significant power in that they know what must be done by law and what was done by convention previously. They may see their role as running the council despite the councillors, or they may work closely with them. The elected chair (or mayor) usually has a formal role in managing the work of the clerk and appraising their performance, though this function is often neglected or non-existent. The mayor/chair is likely to change every few years, taking with them any continuity in the management of the clerk.

It seems to me this can more or less work in two scenarios. The first is if the clerk runs the show and the councillors do pretty little. This is the traditional model and can be effective if the clerk is competent and the scale of decision making minimal. However, the more the clerk does the less the skills and experience of the councillors are utilised, so it's a missed opportunity and a democratic nonsense.
In the second scenario, the model can work when (and this usually happens by luck) a solid set of councillors are matched with a competent clerk and staff. Fortunately, the second scenario is the one that Frome has enjoyed in recent years, with the added benefit of attracting staff who've been more than simply competent.

DEVELOPING THE NEW IfF
Buddy groups
Recognising the need to get to know each other better and also to bring new councillors up to speed, we developed a 'buddy system'. This placed experienced councillors and new ones in groups of three and encouraged them to meet. This worked really well for some trios, and they met a number of times. Others never really took off, but overall, it was an important initiative. This gave new councillors a safe space to ask 'silly questions', to gain a deeper understanding of the relationship between the council and its officers and how the process of governing works. All too often these questions never get asked, though they have an important role in testing the status quo, which can often need dismantling.

IfF meetings
IfF has met once a month during its existence. These meetings are administered and chaired by an annually-elected convenor. We use small group discussions and feedback on a few key issues and also include an opportunity for each of us to express how we're feeling, both as a councillor and on a personal level. Some people never really liked this second aspect, and it has gently faded out. We still use full group discussions sometimes, but in general, the meetings have become more formal and traditional. Personally, I think this is a pity, but I'm the only one!

Rules for debate
In the monthly IfF meetings, without the constraints of formal council papers to agree or reject, the IfF discussions are often more lively and interesting. However, they're rarely debates in the true sense of the word; they tend to be mainly about sharing information. In contrast, council meetings are the forum for making decisions and in theory the home of rigorous debates.

Alternativet, the Danish political party mentioned elsewhere, has developed six principles for debate. I share these below because a version of these might have helped us, both in the IfF group and in council meetings, to reinvigorate our debates.
- We will openly discuss both the advantages and the disadvantages of a certain argument or line of action
- We will listen more than we speak, and we will meet our political opponents on their own ground
- We will emphasize the core set of values that guide our arguments
- We will acknowledge when we have no answer to a question or when we make mistakes
- We will be curious about each and every person with whom we are debating

- We will argue openly and factually as to how The Alternativet's political vision can be realized.

Without a constant reminder of process, it is easy to slip back into more traditional behaviour, not seeing the people excluded by that process.

Lead councillors and other roles

In an attempt to ensure each councillor could play as full a role as they want and to get the best from each of us we took three steps:

1) Increasing the number of formal roles for councillors.
2) Creating the role of sponsor.
3) Removing committees and establishing panels.

Increasing the number of formal roles for councillors

We increased the number of formal roles by adding a deputy leader of the council and a deputy convenor of IfF. We encouraged nominations with the following criteria:

- Do you/they have the experience and skills required, and the time available?
- Will your overall choice maintain continuity in providing staff with the support and guidance they need?
- Have you/they read the job description?
- Will you/they be able to represent the Town Council and Frome at all levels?
- Have you/they left their ego at home?

Anyone wishing to stand could make a short pitch to express an interest in a particular post, with a time limit of three minutes. This was followed by a secret ballot. After the results were announced, there was then a 'sensible conversation' to reshuffle people who'd been elected in more than one position and in an attempt to meet all desires. This worked as far as I know, though it is the nature of life that some people may have been unhappy and never revealed this.

I've provided the job descriptions for the key roles in an Appendix 2. Both the 'official' ones that made their way into the standing orders and some unofficial comments of my own on what the roles really entail. Setting out what each role is intended to achieve reduces the potential for confusion and misuse of power. It's been important to remind ourselves every now and then that this group, meeting as IfF, can't make decisions, even when most of the councillors were present. So outside of the IfF roles the choices for council positions were technically only proposals, and voting took place in a council meeting later.

Creating the role of sponsor

Beyond expanding formal roles, we looked to link each councillor to specific areas of interest and responsibility. This role had two aims. Firstly, to utilise each councillor's skills and experiences; secondly, to give them a real role that would keep them hooked in. We called them 'sponsors' and later 'lead councillors'. Initially, this worked well, with the key member of staff in that work area meeting the sponsor regularly. This provided a way in which information and ideas could flow without conflicting views from councillors inundating staff. In some cases, councillors held regular meetings with a number of staff. For example, I met monthly with the resilience manager and her manager.

As these sponsors and their roles bedded in, they reported back to the IfF group meetings. In theory, at least, this kept us all up to date and allowed us to comment in a way that formal council meetings couldn't.

The full sponsor's job description can be found in the Appendix 2.

Removing the committees and establishing panels

The third move aimed to bring all 17 councillors into the mix was to remove the committee structure. We'd previously reduced the large number of committees and subcommittees to two: one aimed at covering the internal workings of the council and the other, the work we do with the outside community.

However, with all councillors wanting to be involved, and a desire to further increase the levels of participation and real engagement, it made sense to make some changes. We disbanded the committee structure, increased the number of full council meetings to one a month, and instigated a series of panels on specific subjects. (I'll come on to the panels in Chapter 5.) It was quite easy to do. Below is a recommended wording for the motion: *"With the exception of the planning committee to suspend the current committee structure until such time as a new committee structure is agreed. In the interim period give the town clerk delegated authority, in consultation with the chair of the council, to deal with day-to-day decisions."*

While the panels were a great success, abandoning the committees was not. The papers for one full meeting seemed to arrive before the previous minutes were out, and there was simply too much on agendas. We returned to the original committee structure a year later.

When we reformed the two committees mentioned above, we ensured that each had delegated powers to make decisions. This is crucial. Many councils have committees that have to take recommendations to main meetings for ratification. This both undermines the powers of the committee and pushes all decisions to one central point. It also clogs up the ability of the council to make speedy decisions.

The Planning Advisory Group

For Frome, planning decisions are made at the district level and at the county level where there is no district. However, most town councils have planning committees, which take up most of their agenda. This causes endless confusion amongst the good people who come to complain about their neighbour's garage door plans or to discuss more major issues like significant developments.

We decided to come clean and try to clarify where the power really lay. We disbanded the planning committee and established a planning advisory group (PAG). This has been a great success. It still meets often in order to make comments to the district. Generally, these comments are in relation to large and significant developments in the town. We use staff and sometimes consultants to properly inform the group. Smaller or 'personal' planning issues are steered to the district councillors and their meetings, where the issues actually need to be heard and are decided. These PAG meetings are very open, with an informed introduction from the chair, then lively, engaged discussion. By moving to issues of wider concern and away from the personal ones, they've become another way the council has properly engaged with residents.

Party/conferences: what works and what doesn't

I doubt many town councils go beyond a rare away-day for councillors. IfF has had an annual party/conference (a joke about our not being a political party but still being able to party that I've failed to explain innumerable times). These have been fundamentally important in creating the foundations from which our ambitions have emerged. With 17 councillors this involved not just renting a holiday cottage for the weekend, but much larger setups.

As always, we've used facilitators who've been supporters of IfF and who have professional skills and knowledge of the world in which the council operates. The events have run over a weekend, with some people coming a bit early and/or leaving late and others ensuring a good 24 hours of overlap with an evening together. What works is the opportunity to really take time to look at some of the key strategic issues we face. I doubt, for example, we'd have faced up to austerity without the space to develop so many creative ideas. It's also a great way in which to get to know people better, especially those from different spaces and places in Frome. Recognising that we have more in common than not has been crucial to putting into practice some of the more challenging aspects of our Ways of Working.

What doesn't work is that this kind of event is a space that not all people find easy to work in. From the 2015 council group there were always a couple of people who didn't come at all and others came but with a lesser level of engagement. On top of that, because some people have a set of in-jokes and shared moments, there's further potential for alienation.

I don't have a simple answer to all this. We possibly could have found more ways to enable people to come for the parts that worked for them, leaving the rest. And this is also where I realise the IfF councils have been ridiculously ambitious in some ways. How can we possibly feel disappointed that it's a struggle to get 17 people to come away together, work over a weekend and pay for the privilege?

Consultation

The follow up to the Localism Act has spawned many reports and studies. There are also organisations funded to try and make the legislation more effective. Because of Frome's higher profile, we've been invited to contribute evidence on a number of occasions, most notably to the Commission on the Future of Localism and the Forum for the Future's 'Civil Society Futures'. This has been an opportunity to share our experiences as to the failure of localism. It's also enabled us to showcase how a model and strategy like Frome's has the potential to create a platform for much more radical initiatives for reforming council/town relationships.

I'm fairly cynical as to what happens to these time consuming and expensive reports and studies. In one case there was a 'targeted pilot' set up to take on the recommendations that emerged. Unfortunately, as it was woefully under-resourced the recommendations remained just that, recommendations. I'll come on to real alternatives in the final chapter, but my experience is that the system is far too entrenched to accept all but the most minor of changes.

Attracting others to Frome

Of greater interest has been the way in which Frome's higher political profile has attracted a range of people and initiatives to the town. Those individuals include people who have moved here directly because they see IfF's existence as symbolic of the kind of place they want to live. We've also attracted visits from the well known, like George Monbiot and Carne Ross, who have readily accepted invitations whereas they might not have before.

Frome is also seen as a place where new ideas are welcomed. We've accepted initiatives from outside of Frome to look at things like Rights for the River Frome, new currency and banking ideas, and routes towards viable local energy production. The fact that initiatives have been brought to us has meant that we can test these ideas with little input of time or money.

Real, visible change, such as that brought about by IfF, also attracts academics. There are at least two PhDs about local councils in their later stages of research at present. Interesting initial comments from Jason Leman's research on the role of local councils include this: *"... my view on local councils is that they can help create virtuous spirals. They can help solve local problems through connecting and supporting local groups and individuals, providing spaces to talk and think about solutions and gathering or mobilising resources to act."*

He also lists a range of positives and negatives related to IfF's practice, and these will be important to look at once his work is finished.

Amy Burnett has now completed her PhD thesis: 'Planning for Transitions: a case study of Frome'. It explores how 'formalised' policies, practices, and spheres of governance relate to more 'bottom-up' activities in the pursuit of new models of socio-political development in and around the planning process'.

The work provides a significant analysis of the role of cultural qualities and of key individuals in forming an environment for positive change. A book on the topic is in the pipeline.

The catchy title of Kris Fowler's MSc thesis is: 'Tessellating Dissensus: Resistance, Autonomy and Radical Democracy – can transnational municipalism constitute a counterpower to liberate society from neoliberal capitalist hegemony?'

The following extract summarises its aims: 'Learning from experiences in Frome, Barcelona and around the world to contend that the municipality is the organisational scale best able to bring about a new economic logic for the transition to a sane, sustainable, free and compelling 21st century life through truly democratic and authentically political processes.'

Frome also features as one of 50 municipalist cities in a new guide to the movement. In all these academic works, IfF has played an important role in stimulating new ideas. Arguably, the influence of IfF has been much greater than its size would suggest.

What next for IfF?

It may be that IfF's work is done. It's important that before deciding to re-emerge before an election, that question is seriously asked. It's hard to believe we'd return to the conflict-ridden stagnation of the past, but complacency could easily be the downfall of radical politics in Frome.

In both 2015 and 2019 the struggle for party power led to some candidates who had little to offer except their party membership. It would be all too easy for IfF to think they have a right to rule, and for some terrible publicity on one issue to let back in those whose allegiance is primarily to their national party.

At present, I can see no obvious alternative to the 'IfF way', which is to bring together the best people and enable them to act ambitiously.

The Birmingham University Public Service Academy's report 'The 21st Century Councillor' quotes two council leaders: *"... how do we get more people with the ability to think about these complex issues in local government?... The kind of people you need to do that are successful business people or those with professional managerial jobs, people who've got a good level of education, who've been successful in different kind of things.'"*

"... you don't want to make it too professional so that it's not accessible for people. We come back into that argument then about having working class people representing communities you know, you've got to have that balance haven't you?"

To date, IfF has been hugely successful in attracting a range of people with great skills and experience, something political parties cannot. Then, having brought people together, the use of some kind of Ways of Working enables that group to meet its full potential.

The next chapter provides the 'proof of the pudding'. It sets out what has changed in the council over the last four years and what it's achieved, beyond its minimum requirement to provide allotments and hold one meeting a year.

5. What Frome Town Council did: part 1

The newly-renovated Frome Town Hall

THE COUNCIL STRUCTURES AND SYSTEMS

Chapter 4 focussed on changes that happened to Independents for Frome from 2011; the next two chapters look at changes in practice in the council over that period.

As all the councillors were from IfF, there is overlap in who can take the credit for the many changes that happened. However, irrespective of who initiated what, this chapter aims to cover initiatives and projects that any other council could adopt, even the very traditional, vanilla varieties.

Part 1 covers changes we made to how the council carries out its work. Part 2 covers what's actually happened on the ground. It's an unashamedly long list, because I want to encourage others who are still stuck in the belief that a council at this level is limited in scope. I have aimed to give a taste of key activity in each area, rather than attempt to cover everything that happened (this would be a standalone book). I've also included some of those things that didn't work out. I do this in part to learn lessons but also to encourage risk taking, which will inevitably result in some things not going as planned.

The status quo

I could write pages on the horror stories that have been shared with me by councillors, staff and the public relating to their town and parish councils. But I have also heard some great tales of ambitious initiatives working well. Sadly, the majority of stories that I hear are the former. Some because the council is corrupt or dysfunctional but mostly because it's trudging along, not doing anything of consequence. This isn't surprising given the challenge of attracting anyone to an often tedious voluntary role, where it's incredibly hard to bring about change quickly. What infuriates me most, and I've touched on this already, is when people confuse tradition with stagnation. By all means have a mayoral mace if you must, just please don't confuse waving it around with good governance.

For example, the then mayor of Frome, Toby Eliot, was invited to a Mayor's Civic Reception in a neighbouring town. It was on a Friday evening, and 110 people had gathered in a brightly lit, modern hall in the middle of town. All the neighbouring mayors and councillors from both tiers were present, together with town council staff. All were formally dressed in black tie and all were sitting down to a mediocre, silver service, three-course meal. Overlong speeches were made, which mainly involved thanking other people in the hall, punctuated by everyone having to stand to welcome the new mayor, to drink toasts to said mayor and of course, toast the Queen.

There's nothing intrinsically wrong with all of this, except perhaps it was funded by a cash-strapped town council. In addition, the majority of the residents, who'd paid for the extravaganza through their council tax, undoubtedly didn't have a clue it was going on and were extremely unlikely ever to be invited. It felt to Toby as though they were in an endless cycle of always doing what had been done without understanding or questioning why.

On the plus side, the whole experience was a very positive reinforcement of how different Frome Town Council was.

CHANGING THE RELATIONSHIPS WITHIN THE COUNCIL AND BEYOND

Within the council

If people don't have genuine responsibility, we can't expect them to act responsibly. The first meeting of Frome's new council had a six point agenda, with clear explanations of key points. The clerk explained the role of Frome Town Council (FTC) and where the parish sector sits compared with other tiers of local government. He explained that the precept was the amount raised from council tax payers in Frome and was the bulk of FTC's income. The clerk then introduced the staff. He went on to suggest that it was good practice to review the standing orders at the start of a new administration and recommended that they were suspended. Also that it was also good practice for a new administration to produce a new corporate strategy based on the needs and aspirations of the community as a whole, and that it was necessary to undertake a robust engagement exercise in order to achieve this.

Compare this to the horror story that greeted Monmouth Town Council's new independents: an agenda with 30 items, including the impressive '... to review the council's procedures for handling requests made under the Freedom of information act 2000 and data protection act 1998 (SO 5jxvi)...'

Changing the rules

The standing orders, in effect the rules, of a council contain some edicts that cannot be changed without parliamentary approval. But the vast majority of what is in there is guidance. It can, and usually should, be dragged into the 21st century. Dom Newton of Ideal Bradford, the independents who run Bradford on Avon council said that their first act was to go through the standing orders and divide them into three groups: the statutory, which have to be kept, those that are sensible to keep, and those that can be done away with or substantially altered. He then went on to check that those labelled 'statutory act' really were a legal requirement.

The very first moment the council meets is the time to act. Once standing orders are agreed and committees have been settled you won't be able to revisit them for ages and may well slip into just going with what was originally there. Suspending the standing orders and taking a few weeks to adjust them was easy to do using the following words: 'Under section 25a of standing orders, suspend standing orders, review them and agree any amendments at an extraordinary council meeting on 10 June.'

Later on, we revisited the whole set of rules and pared them down to a bare minimum to allow maximum flexibility. Too often complexity and detail gives power to those in the know. In the context of *Flatpack Democracy* this especially applies to town clerks, some of whom have been known to use the standing orders to bore everyone into a stupor, leaving them to achieve their own ends.

Portishead Independents said 'their first act will be to burn the standing orders' if they took power in 2019. They did take power and have enthusiastically set about making changes, starting with leaving behind formal dress and being addressed as 'Councillor'.

Informality

How we talk to each other and what we wear changes our relationships both within the council and with the public. In Frome, the lack of political opposition or a traditional past made it easier to reduce the formal aspect of how we did things even more than in our first administration. Of course, informality doesn't mean that serious business cannot be transacted in a proper manner. Where else in day-to-day transactions, except perhaps the courts, are you told that only certain people can speak and for how long, how you must address those in charge and how you must dress?

A few words of warning

I comment frequently on how important the informal culture IfF has developed has been in changing the relationship between the council and the community. But this is a personal view. Sometimes a more formal setup might help members of the public engage in a particular process. Recognising that our informal culture might be a challenge to some, we did implement ways to help people in meetings. For example, we would ask if there were any new people present and if there were, explain to them how the meeting would work.

It's also easy to assume the clerk is a supporter of the old ways because they explain the rules to you. That's their job. Many would be more than happy to help to change the rules. It is so much better to retain a good working relationship with the clerk, recognising and understanding what they're legally responsible for before attacking them for not changing things.

Whilst we've pushed hard to avoid being bound by rules and processes, there is a risk that their lack can allow for traditional patterns of domination to reassert themselves. Sometimes the pushing away of rules with the aim of encouraging non-hierarchical ways of working in fact allows unspoken hierarchies to operate. Dropping rules and processes doesn't solve the issue of people dominating things, and perhaps sometimes it's about having different kinds of rules and processes that make for equity. All of which is an argument for the regular use of an external observer or facilitator who can help spot these issues early and find ways to redirect the process.

HOW WE RUN MEETINGS
Full council and committee meetings

Getting meetings to work for councillors, staff and the public is challenging. Traditional committee meetings are often incomprehensible (to staff, councillors and of course the long suffering public). They can be overly long, convoluted and hidebound by self-imposed rules. The layouts and formats of agendas have often not changed for years and don't reflect the possibilities of modern presentation techniques. Few councils use videos, pictures or easy-to-read projection techniques. The public often feel excluded at meetings; this is exacerbated if the councillors all sit together in a bunch, sideways on, or even worse, with their back to the public.

We were determined to address some of these problems. Over the last four years we have refined a series of improvements and techniques. Some have been more successful than others, and not all will be appropriate for all councils or all situations.

Layout

To start with, let's look at the simplest improvement: the physical layout of a council meeting. In fact, we've never hit upon a truly successful approach or complete agreement, though no one would want to return to layout where there's a table of councillors sitting separately from public. The basic premise is that councillors need to be able to discuss matters and make decisions, and they need to be seen to be doing so in a transparent and inclusive way. This has informed our two different meeting layouts:

First, the broad horseshoe with councillors facing one another and the public, located at the open end of the horseshoe. In this way all contributors can be seen and only some of the public have their backs to one another.

A more radical version of this is that all except the chair and the clerk share round tables with councillors who are dotted around the room. Councillors can vote by holding aloft a very visible card. This breaks down barriers of communication almost completely. As a result, it can make chairing more challenging, as members of the public feel quite able to speak at any moment. However, I've been hugely impressed at how rarely the public abuse this level of inclusion. The fully open format does, however, make it less easy for councillors to debate matters amongst themselves.

We should also examine the layout of a normal council agenda, which tends to get everything off to a terrible start. Typefaces are often archaic and it's difficult to see how and when business is to be transacted. Often it immediately launches into some gobbledegook about 'members being summoned' etc. We've attempted to simplify the front page of the agenda so it can be used as an invitation. It normally contains a picture of a relevant item and lists the business at hand using words like 'an update', 'to approve' or 'for information'. Many updates are verbal. All items of substance have a standard format, including a summary of what the report is about, why it's here and what is expected of councillors.

We keep agendas short. I've seen agendas of 100 pages or more (yes, really, 100 plus pages). In contrast, we usually have 10 items or fewer and 20 pages in total would be considered excessive. We delegate to the staff who are experienced in producing usable and informative agendas.

Engagement

This is probably the most contentious element amongst the visitors we have from other councils. We have a strong belief that not all knowledge lies with councillors, or staff for that matter, and better decisions are made if we can tap into local expertise. To facilitate this we don't restrict public discussion or presentations to 15 minutes at the beginning of the meeting. Whilst we ask at the start if anyone wants to speak about matters not on the agenda, we prefer to engage in discussion with those who are interested in a particular item when it arises in the meeting. Strictly speaking, business should be suspended to allow discourse by the public, but this is where common sense is allowed to prevail.

Sometimes on interesting or contentious issues we break the room into small groups and allow discussion and feedback. This helps to inform councillors and puts some of our ideas to an immediate test. Lots of new ideas have emerged from this way of doing things, and we may use this technique when we genuinely don't have an answer to a knotty problem.

When there's something really controversial, we've taken this to a separate public meeting and used professional facilitators. This means a decision by councillors can't be taken as it's not a formal meeting. However, we invariably adopt the direction taken at a later official council meeting.

Notice I have used the words 'facilitate meetings' rather than 'chair'. Formal chairing of meetings, working down each agenda item and taking comments from those who raise their hand is much easier than an evolving, relaxed style of facilitating meetings. We've been lucky in finding chairs well able to manage a more informal process.

Publicity, visuals and broadcasts

Agendas are placed on our Facebook page and website, and followed up on Twitter as soon as they're dispatched to councillors and a wide list of those who may be (or should be) interested. The town now boasts 14 physical information boards (made of recycled plastics) on which agendas are posted. These are maintained by community volunteers who live nearby. Individual items are also picked out and highlighted on social media. For a while we also advertised meetings in the local weekly newspaper.

At all council meetings we encourage sketching, recording, tweeting, filming and anything else you can think of.

As a society that likes its information in a more visual form and as the written word becomes less prominent, we need to keep in step. So we try to make visual presentations to summarise the main points of a proposition and recommendations. We use pictures and maps or merely images that give amusing takes on local issues. This epitomises the need to balance making good decisions with an underlying principle of 'keep it light'.

Our meetings have been broadcast by the local radio station Frome FM. At the time of writing one of our most disappointing failures has been technical problems with the expensive live broadcast equipment. Apparently a soundless broadcast doesn't make the meeting any more interesting!

We also try to have an easy-to-follow summary of the meeting published by the next day so interested parties know what has happened. With all this, the numbers of people attending are exceptional in comparison to elsewhere. Even so, unless there's a really significant planning application or contentious issue, there may well be only ten members of the public present. My view is that this will never significantly change and we will only get real engagement when we go to where the people are. Hence the use of panels and the People's Budget, which this council has placed at the heart of creating real engagement.

We aim for meetings to last no more than two hours; relatively short, interesting or even entertaining meetings help you get good attendance from councillors and the public.

In conclusion, the flexible and continually evolving way the council now runs meetings works well for Frome. It's been well worth experimenting and allowing councillors to decide on what they feel most comfortable with and what achieves the differing aims. For other councils, what this comes down to is whether the meetings are for councillors to make decisions alone or part of a process in which councillors encourage public participation in order to guide them to a decision. A visiting resident from Desborough who attended a council meeting said: *"Firstly, thank you so much for meeting me last night and welcoming me to Frome. Now I know the way to host a Town Council meeting, which is not rocket-science but sadly lacking not only in Desborough but I suspect in many, many other councils. I really enjoyed some of the simple methods used to engage with the public and the fact that all councillors contributed; members of the public were respectfully addressed; those presenting (Gloria, Ian and Chris) addressed the public rather than the councillors. No egos, everyone listening closely, nice people. For me personally (and possibly strangely for some!) an enjoyable evening I was pleased to witness so thank you once again."*

Working meetings

Many people who attend Frome Town Council meetings have been surprised that the informality described percolates through to all aspects of the council. This can need explaining to outsiders. I was at a meeting recently where a county councillor stopped things early on to ask, 'Is this a committee? Does it make decisions? Who's the chair and who's taking minutes?' All of these are reasonable questions; the important elements were all in place, just hidden in layers of normal, real life behaviour, which was probably why the councillor was confused.

Panels

Blurring the edges between council and community has been at the heart of the council's aspirations. While the new strategy could identify the broad direction of policy, there were areas of work where we, as councillors, recognised the need to bring additional expertise into the picture. 'Expertise' might mean professional experience and skills or, more than likely, it meant that someone had personal experience of the issue because of where they lived, or what they did.

With half an eye on some radical ideas that were emerging from Spain, we designed panels. These are based on the Spanish process of holding large public meetings that effectively created policy that politicians then adopted.

Our model was not quite so radical. It involved setting up a short series of meetings focussed on one particular area of work where we needed public input into the broad strategic direction to take. Our panels cover elements of a 'Task and Finish Group' and also of a 'People's Assembly' in that they're well-facilitated open meetings addressing single issues. The initial subject areas were Keep Frome Clean; Wellbeing; the Town Centre; and Sports and Leisure. We later added the Performing Arts Panel.

Panels were set out to be short term. Once their work was done, they disbanded. They set out to identify concerns, test imaginative and interesting solutions and make recommendations to the council. This leads to commissioning projects to be undertaken by the town council staff and the creation of partnerships with community organisations.

Central to the ethos was that the outcomes of the panels really would be taken up by the council and incorporated into work plans and budgets. Without this we'd slide back into another loop of consultation leading to nothing but increased cynicism. The formation, remit and timetable of each new panel was approved by the council so we could get a broad spread of topics and some quick results.

The panels were open to the public and their formation and meetings well advertised. Whilst 'experts' were invited to contribute and sit on the panel, the whole point was that panels would be led by, and populated mainly by, non-councillors – thus recognising and tapping into the infectious enthusiasm and local knowledge of residents. Each panel has a lead councillor and a member of staff to support the process, who might also facilitate meetings or bring in additional expertise.

The panels were a great success. In terms of bringing in new people, the Sport and Leisure panel was extraordinary. It met in the football, rugby and cricket clubs, all of which, incidentally, had bars! These well-defined and carefully-facilitated meetings brought more than 50 new people to each meeting. I was greatly impressed by all the participants' seriousness and the way they readily acknowledged the limitations of the council's power; we weren't asked to build a new skating rink or a swimming pool, and so it was easy for the council to adopt various proposals, many of which have now happened.

Three of the panels actually went on to form 'forums', because they valued the networking aspect of meeting so much. These continue to meet regularly, though not very often, and are valuable ways for staff and councillors to re-engage on specific areas of work. It should be noted, however, that some staff have reservations about how panels morphed into forums. Potentially, too much prolonged discussion could create an ever-growing workload for staff and thus undermine the original intent to provide clear, quickly-informed strategy.

The original thought was that we might tackle 20 or so different topics over the next four years. After the initial five, no more have emerged. Mainly, this is because we underestimated the amount of time they would take to run and to set the recommendations into motion. The idea was that by only having monthly council meetings, and no committees, staff could focus on the panels, but we underestimated the workload of the main meetings. I hope that panels are reintroduced in later councils, perhaps in a more phased way. They could certainly be part of a strategic approach to better public engagement.

Frome's panels may be the precursor to a sophisticated Citizen's Assembly. As I leave the council, there are plans to establish one of these to ask what the climate and environmental emergency really means for Frome. A Citizen's Assembly would seek around 50 members of the public, carefully selected through sortition, to hear expert advice over three or four days. Behind this is a belief that a small number of well-informed people will make a better decision than a large number who are less, or wrongly, informed. What a pity no one thought of this before the Brexit referendum.

A NEW STRATEGY

The 2015 council inherited a strategy, work plan and budget from the 2011 administration. These could of course have been changed, but it made good sense to take some time to look at what was behind those ideas and then adjust them to enable what the new council wanted to achieve.

In my view, strategy should be the councillors' main focus of attention. Far too many councils micromanage staff instead of standing back and looking at what will lead to real change. While the 2015 strategy was produced by the IfF councillors, I have included comment on the process in this chapter because its creation and final format entailed close work with senior staff. Ultimately it forms the basis for work plans and budgets for the entire period of the council, so it's fundamentally a joint document. The strategy agreed by the 2015 IfF councillors is, in my opinion, a really solid document. Its introduction reads: '*This Strategy sets out the broad vision and ethos of the council. This vision sits within both the wider and the local context. It provides the detail of where we want to get to and how we should get there. It aims to provide the framework within which the community, other councils, the voluntary sector and business can interrelate with Frome Town Council over the next four years. The strategy provides enough detail to prepare the annual work plans and budgets – while being flexible enough to seize new opportunities as they arise.*'

I include the whole strategy on the *Flatpack Democracy* website for the aficionados of strategies and a summary below. The strategy establishes that everything the council does, will do and will support broadly falls into the following three areas:
1) **Wellbeing**: a flourishing and active community of people and organisations working together
2) **Prosperity**: a thriving business community, connected with each other and with the town, providing employment and prosperity.
3) **Environmental sustainability**: covering the attractiveness, variety and accessibility of the town's green spaces and an increased focus on renewable energy, energy efficiency, waste reduction, and community transport.

The strategy document goes on to set out how the council will approach business and the things that will always apply to its actions:

- Unconstrained by a Political agenda, the council will be bold.
- Participation and engagement are central to the thinking of the council.
- Others will be enabled to be successful.
- The council will campaign, lobby and lead.
- The council will practice what it preaches.

The People's Budget

For some reason 'Participator Budgeting' is often hard to say. Some bright spark noticed PB can also stand for the People's Budget, so that's what we renamed work to enable the people to make budget decisions. PB is not a Frome idea by a long way, but it has become an important element of the way many councils and governments engage with the public. In Paris, for example, around 5% of capital expenditure (€100m p.a.) is spent in this way.

There are two main reasons to let the people make budget decisions. Firstly, with a good process, they're more than likely to make better decisions than the elected representatives; secondly, it's a way to break down political divisions and scepticism. And there are a shed load of other benefits too, from increasing engagement with the council and each other to the experience of working constructively with conflict. Mayor Councillor Toby Eliot took the lead on making this happen in Frome with three kinds of initiative.

In the first experiment, the council invited people to vote for different options on the tricky question of toilets in the park. The old toilets had been repeatedly vandalised, adding to their maintenance costs of £20,000 a year. These were the options present to the people of Frome:

1) Give up on the toilets.
2) Build something near the existing cafe reasonably cheaply.
3) Build a new cafe and toilets, using the existing maintenance budget to service a larger loan.

The council advertised the choice and process widely, and over 1,000 people voted. The result was a vote for a new building, but the process of engaging so many people in thinking through the options and considering costs was really more important. This model has developed into giving the public an annual choice between three different projects (of around £10,000 each). Key to the process is the council could live with any result and that whatever option is chosen happens quickly. Last year the people voted for a new town orchard, which was planted within a few months and has been both hugely popular and also avoided vandalism, possibly because of a sense of community ownership.

In parallel, around £25,000 a year has been offered to local non-profit groups to fund events in the coming year. In this case, they all make a short video to present to an audience of around 100 in the football club. Those bidding also answer questions. It's been very rewarding watching the level of engagement at these events: people ask tough questions of the bidders and are able to really take on board what their choices will mean for the community.

The results of this process? A cycle-powered cinema, a firework event, a disability and diversity day, and a seriously offbeat fitness event have all been funded. Because these events all happen just a few months after the public have chosen for the council to fund them, there's a visceral connection between people's choices and things happening. Would I, with my councillor hat on, have made these choices? No. Does that matter? No. And in the case of the hugely successful fireworks event, which I'd previously been against, I was happy to eat my hat, because the wider public expressed a desire that outweighed my concerns.

It will depend on future councils as to whether this initiative is continued, but for me it's been an important and integral part of changing the council's relationship with the public in a very positive way.

STAFFING
The relationship
Frome councillor Mel Usher says in a speech he gave to the Society of Local Clerks annual meeting entitled Great Myths that: *"It may look from the outside as if the councillors decide policy and the staff carry it out. This misapprehension leads to confusion and dishonesty which will persist in this sector as long as it is perpetuated. At best, there is an interactive, complementary relationship. When there is an imbalance, with strong staff and weak councillors, or the other way around, it always comes back to bite you. Without a solid relationship there are endless rows: town clerks rarely get sacked for incompetence but for falling out."*

We've spent a lot of time recognising this in Frome (largely through Mel's previous experience of these matters). Councillors and staff invariably meet together to determine how to handle issues, with briefings on how things might progress combined with numerous informal sessions. This underpins a mutual respect in

Frome that's been behind much of what's been achieved. Of course, there have been exceptions, but I believe this solid and respectful relationship is essentially why we've managed to attract and retain staff of exceptional quality.

Once the quality is there, it's possible for staff to take more and more responsibility for ongoing work, keeping councillors well informed but without having to seek permission. This is a balance, however, and there have been moments when staff have taken initial ideas from a councillor and turned them into a project more quickly than might have been wise. But in general this is preferable to hanging back waiting for permission. With a political opposition I suspect this would have been picked up on and used as a stick to beat us with; arguably, fear of staff taking too much initiative is why councils so often end up doing very little.

The structure and staff

The 2011 IfF council set out to have as flat and horizontal a structure as possible, but to date have not really achieved this. The 2015 council created something closer to that aspiration. Frome has a town clerk and deputy at the top, a team of six managers in the middle and a layer of project officers and support staff below. It's a considerable regret to me that whilst five out of six of the managers are women, the top two posts are held by men. It was hard to see how to change this largely inherited situation, but it is giving out a poor message.

The funding constraints are such that it's never going to be possible to compete with the open market in how these posts are paid. We've tried to counter this by providing a place that's a pleasure to work in and salaries and conditions at the higher end of the scale. In addition, the council is a registered 'Living Wage Employer', which impacts on its choices of contractors as well as the staff. As a result, the staff seem to greatly enjoy being part of a working environment they themselves have created.

At the end of this council period there will be 21 staff. In keeping with the strategic aim to practice what we preach, the council has also taken on a series of apprentices. So far this has been hugely successful, with all of them going on to employment. The management layer, mentioned above, covers responsibility for planning and development, resilience, the environment, wellbeing, marketing and communications, and the business manager. The three project workers started off in non-specific roles, but then became linked to the work of specific managers. I'm not convinced about this, as I'd have thought they'd enjoy some variety and benefit from having a range of experiences.

The three-tiered council structure then partially breaks down; there's another layer that includes the town rangers and town hall steward, all of whom are paid less and have fewer direct responsibilities. It would be good to find ways to remedy this.

The rangers

The largest increase in staffing has come with the rangers team. The council initially had a small group of groundsmen who primarily looked after the park and plantings in the town. Their role and what they were prepared to take on was strictly limited. How well I remember asking, out of hours and in vain, for help when the town Christmas tree started falling over into the road.

Over the last few years the groundsmen have been replaced by five rangers who are, in part, community workers. We recognise that the rangers are the face of the council in the community, and as such we have deliberately employed people able to listen and respond to comments as well as carry out essential maintenance on an ever-increasing estate. The rangers' work now covers a whole variety of tasks, from ensuring the notice board volunteers are doing their job, to helping provide equipment for events and street parties, to working with schools to place bird and bat boxes. Our experience is that this has benefited everyone: the rangers enjoy doing more than just cutting grass and the public have clearly appreciated their increased involvement in the community.

Here's a note of thanks we received: *"A big Thank You to the Frome Town Council ranger who retrieved a wheelie bin which had been chucked in the river Frome. Some jokers decided to take it for a journey on Saturday night down Chateau Gontier Walk and tip it into the river. This morning David managed to fish the wheelie bin out of the river and also cleaned up all of the smashed glass. Please pass on our gratitude to David. What he did was above and beyond the call of duty."*

Finally, another example of where the town council has operated at its best. A group from the community expressed a clear need for a Changing Places Toilet (a toilet accessible to those with extra special needs). Town councillors provided support in negotiations with the district, who are responsible for toilets. After many months they agreed to use a vacant building and provide maintenance, allocating some money from funds already destined for the town. But unfortunately, there was still a £10,000 shortfall. Frome Town Council creatively reallocated some budgets and used some reserves to provide the £10K, and all of this was arranged in a few days. What this required was a strong community group, a town councillor to provide support, and flexible, imaginative staff looking for ways to say 'yes' rather than 'no'.

A final thought

I've quoted Mel Usher a number of times in this section, and this is no coincidence. Most successful, independent-led councils have one or two individuals who drive the process forward, at least initially. Mel's experience as the chief executive of South Somerset District Council, followed by innumerable advisory roles, has been incredibly important in keeping IfF ambitious and focussed.

I've included some edited notes from a talk he gave on the role of councils in Appendix 3. While not all of this applies to Frome, or what the council has changed in the last four years, it does provide insight into the thinking behind much of the council's direction, and as such it's well worth a read.

What Frome Town Council did: part 2

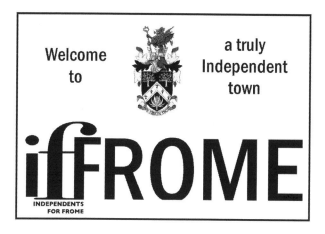

What actually happened

What the outside world thinks of Frome has significantly changed over the last few years; I think it's fair to say that many residents believe it's a more enriching place to live than it used to be. Of course, this isn't only due to the work of the council, but it's definitely played a central role. Some of the newspaper Best Place to Live awards (*The Times, The Telegraph* and *The Guardian,* for example) are to be taken with a pinch of salt as the interested work of the estate agents.

The Guardian's article 'Let's Move to Frome' says "*You want community? You got it (it's the capital of so called Flatpack Democracy...*" was just looking to sell houses. In contrast, the National Great Town Award (Urbanism Awards 2016) fielded a proper set of unbiased judges. They noted in their citation a key element of Frome's renaissance: 'The fact that the town council has established a progressive, risk taking and supportive authority that in the eyes of the assessors genuinely cares about the town and its communities.'

The council itself won Council of the Year at the National Association of Local Councils' (NALC) first ever Star Council Awards in 2015, along with being runner up with Project of the Year for our energy and recycling work. If you add in our winning NALC's Council of the Week on one occasion and Most Proactive Public Body from Regen SW, you can see Frome really is different.

A new relationship with Civil Society

What most of these award makers will not even know about is the concerted effort by the council to change the relationship between itself and the groups and organisations upon which we increasingly rely to provide a mass of services. Some of the initiatives that started with the first IfF council have been strengthened and expanded during the second administration, with the enthusiastic support of both staff and councillors.

A genuinely symbiotic relationship has grown up between the council and local organisations. The council provides all kinds of support to help start or strengthen organisations, and if necessary, it can help keep things going; however, the ownership, and ultimately the power, remains with those running the organisation. The organisation is not answerable to the council. The work of the group may well form part of the strategic aims of the council, but with limited resources it's impossible to cover all the bases without employing more people or seeking out more expertise and funds.

Consistently, where the council has had a hands-off but supportive stance organisations have built on their independence and viability. Keeping things in Frome has been important too: where groups have tried to form but lacked the links, either historical or personal, to Frome, they've struggled or failed.

The organisations that have thrived in a symbiotic relationship with the council over the last few years are too numerous to mention, but a flavour can be got from these three key examples:

Fair Frome

At an early town council meeting a range of local groups was invited to discuss poverty in the town. This brought into focus some desperate situations. Fair Frome emerged from these discussions, with start-up funds and support to get going, but totally independent of the council. They now provide practical solutions to poverty, such as a food bank and a furniture bank. They also arrange community dining events and campaign on issues related to the causes of poverty. Fair Frome does not rely solely on a large grant from any one organisation, which could jeopardise the charity if that funding was ever lost, instead they raise their money locally. In this way, residents beyond the group of local volunteers and trustees can feel a part of what Fair Frome does.

Fair Housing for Frome (FHfF)

Fair Housing for Frome was an initial beneficiary of a People's Budget Bid in which they asked for funds to really understand housing needs in Frome. Facilitated groups of local people met to discuss the housing crisis, seeking a practical response to the provision of decent, secure, affordable and accessible accommodation for local people on low incomes. This is a perfect example of where the council, while recognising the importance of the issue, could not take it on. The traditional approach of appointing a 'housing officer' could never possibly have had the impact that FHfF has already had. An example would be the attracting of significant grant funding that wouldn't have been available to the council.

What the council can do is provide space for a worker, access to training and networking, and small targeted grants. All this goes to tackle an area from which the district and county have withdrawn and occupy a space most town councils would feel unable to enter.

Health Connections Mendip (HCM)

HCM has become the best known of the projects we've supported; it's achieved national recognition and has been extensively copied Here, the relationship is more tenuous and less attributable but I believe the link is clear. HCM was created after Dr Helen Kingston from the Frome Medical Practice sought to find a way to support patients in a more holistic fashion. HCM was set up to enable GPs to prescribe the engagement of a patient with an appropriate community group. Crucially, they have 'Health Connectors', who hold your hand between prescription and action.
The organisation is funded by the Clinical Commissioning Group, and the town council provides an additional £10,000 per annum to part-fund one staff member, who trains and co-ordinates the second layer of the system – the 'community connectors'. A community connector is someone trained to signpost individuals to relevant health groups and organisations.

The connectors help people with any kind of health issue in two ways. Firstly, they link them and their carers to health groups, usually of people with a similar problem. (The project has massively increased the number, range and capacity of these groups to include a hearing support cafe, a leg ulcer club, an MS exercise group and so on.)

Secondly, the connectors signpost people to the broader network of groups and activities in Frome. There are hundreds of these. Some will be fairly easy to find, like groups providing relief for carers or meals to those who cannot leave home; others perhaps less so, like people who volunteer to walk your pet in times of need or the 'Men's Shed', where a large group of men meet regularly to carry out practical tasks while building relationships. (As an aside the Men's Shed has 150 members and has now spawned both a Women's Shed and Young Person's Shed.)

Most of these groups are also on the council's radar. They're supported by the project officers with given training, as well as supported with fundraising and networking. In this way, I think I can safely argue that the significant success of HCM rests, in part, on the work of the council over the last eight years. I believe a fairly short period of intensive, strategic support to the voluntary sector has underpinned the HCM initiative, providing a perfect response to those who ask 'what can a town council possibly do in the case of austerity?'

The benefits of the connector system are not just personal. By early 2018, while emergency admissions to hospitals across Somerset had increased by 29%, incurring a 21% increase in costs, Frome has seen admissions fall by 17%, with a 21% reduction in costs. This represents 5% of the total health budget. No other interventions on record have reduced emergency admissions across a population so effectively.

One resident wrote in to the council about the effect the Talking Café project had had on her life: *"My husband and I have found that the Talking Café has given us both the opportunity to make friends. It has also opened up a huge amount of clubs to join, and given us even more opportunity to widen our friendship group… the Talking Café is an area where we can talk about anything, and laugh. It lifts our spirits. Many older/retired people are isolated, and uninspired, and very sad, as was I. Now I feel happier, and I look forward to meeting others. The Talking Café is a brilliant starting point to the wider community, but the Talking Café in itself is a great club to be in."*

OTHER CHANGES
Wellbeing
Learning from the success of our work with the community and recognising there were parts of Frome society we couldn't reach in more traditional ways, we came up with the concept of wellbeing.

Right back at the start of IfF, the spectre of austerity was hovering over us. Only seven years later, the county, teetering on bankruptcy, is cutting everything to the bone. For Frome, like most places, this means do it yourself or it won't happen. And, as already discussed, we realised this couldn't mean the council employing more people to provide the missing services. Instead, the council had to find clever ways of creating and supporting more community organisations to fill the gaps.

Guided in part by the views of the Wellbeing Forum, our initial approach was to create a new senior post to develop strategic links to other service providers. The post would tap into any remaining activity that the district, county and central government were able to provide. It would also aim to form new links with private or charitable groups as well as the NHS (or is that private now too?).

This strategy proved really challenging: while our work with the community developing new initiatives around sport and health, for example, really took off, we couldn't find a way to get these key major relationships moving, and we had to make the post redundant. However, the focus on wellbeing remains a priority, and the council has taken two directions.

Firstly, the council is running a pilot community development project in one area of the town which has several poverty-related challenges. This is quite a traditional way of doing things, using slow, patient work to empower the community from within. Secondly, the council is focussing on an area particularly hit by county cuts: youth mental health. In line with the council's usual approach, a two-year post has been created with the brief to strengthen, network and support existing community providers in these areas. I see these two projects as focussed experiments to judge carefully where the town council can make a real difference beyond giving wider support to voluntary organisations.

Inputs like those cited above can make a difference but also highlight the limitations of what a town council can really do. To change the system requires both advocacy and campaigning. If the council takes on high-profile campaigning, it's likely to be at loggerheads with the councils above and/or central government. As we've seen with the district council, this can be fun but ultimately unproductive as the town council has so little power. Conversely, if the council heavily supports community organisations engaged in the necessary campaigning and lobbying then that relationship can actually undermine the group's credibility. It can also result in activists being drawn into a cosy relationship with the system, which in turn could reduce their ability to speak out.

I mention these issues to illustrate what challenges a town council (with limited staff capacity and voluntary councillors) faces in stepping into the space created by the lack of input from higher tiers of government.

Stick to the knitting

This second IfF-led council was always going to have a different feel and a different role. The first movers take the leap in the dark, but for their work to have long lasting impact it requires others to follow who consolidate and refine. To underpin this was the Neighbourhood Plan. It was started in the early IfF days and dragged on forever. Eventually it was ratified by the people through a referendum and the various other government organisations that needed to pass it. Elsewhere I've expressed my disappointment at the lack of power and change the Neighbourhood Plan really provided, but what it did do was express the wishes of the people in a range of areas. This in turn has provided a starting point for the new council to operate with confidence.

Below are the main areas in which the second council has carried out this consolidating role.

LAND ACQUISITION AND MANAGEMENT

The vast majority of what the town council has done in recent years is of little concern to the residents compared to their interest in Frome's open spaces. Frome had one big park, a hidden water meadow and a collection of smaller scruffy bits of land. The council has since added 12 new sites, more than doubling the total of public land to a very respectable total of 26 ha (63acres). In most cases, it's taken years of patient work to get these back from the other councils, and in some cases important pieces of land have been bought.

Each of the open spaces now has a carefully-researched management plan, discussed and agreed by the council. There are huge pressures from new housing and infilling, but significant areas of public land are now being thoughtfully maintained. These will help define the feel of Frome for the future.

Saxonvale

Right in the centre of Frome is nearly 5ha of ex-industrial land. With five owners, and an engineering company hanging on to the end, it's been an incredibly difficult area to get developed. In an inspired moment, the council borrowed money and purchased around 0.5ha of the site, partly to protect a skills-training organisation housed there, but mainly to be in the mix of any eventual development. Councillors and staff prodded and persuaded as the rest of the site became more derelict and dangerous. Eventually, the main landowners came together to market the site. In the odd world we now live in, the district council outbid others to buy the site by giving themselves permission to borrow large sums of money and become a property developer.

In early 2019, the town council sold our small section for around £500,000 profit. More importantly, the town council has also negotiated two seats on the development board. This allows the views of the town to be properly represented in a way they definitely wouldn't have been had they not been involved in the sale. If all goes well, this will result in a number of benefits that would not have been achieved if the town were merely lobbying a developer intent solely on profit. Excitingly, these benefits include the very real possibility of all the roofs being covered with solar panels linked to its own micro-grid and the site creating more electricity than it uses. In addition, the skills-training organisation whose home we initially saved through the land purchase will be funded to move to a new site.

Though unseen by the public, all this has, again, taken a huge number of hours of staff and councillor time. However, it's a good example of where the 2015 IfF council has had to knuckle down, with solid, long term benefits to the town.

The Boyle Cross

The desire to be able to cross Frome's town centre main road without being in danger of your life has remained a goal for the last eight years. At last, the steady work is paying off with the inappropriate car-parking area, mentioned earlier, replaced by a paved area. Frome's fountain has also been reactivated, providing endless entertainment to those with a bottle of detergent. In late 2019 we expect the final phases will be rolled out, adding to the 20mph-restriction already in place with a series of new crossings and adjustments to parking.

This project is way outside the normal territory of a town council, and sometimes it's felt like it. In retrospect, the energy and time invested will not have resulted in something we can really be proud of as an exemplar scheme. Certainly, it's a long way from what we first dreamed of, but at least it's way better than it was. Below is a letter from a resident to the deputy town clerk about The Boyle Cross:

"Dear Peter Wheelhouse,
I work from home and my study window overlooks the town centre. I just wanted to let you know that I've seen some really good things taking place as a result of the recent development. I've seen people who use walking sticks reaching the bench and sitting down for a breather to take in the view. Before, there was nowhere suitable to pause. Teenagers meet up at the low wall and socialise for whole afternoons in the holidays, which seems to me to be a good thing because they are right in the thick of town life.

Lots of people are interested in the fountain and it's become somewhere for people to perch and catch up, or sit and think. If they have kids, the space between the fountain and the bench becomes a play area. "You probably know all of this from your surveys but I just wanted to email to add to the congratulations – the centre is more attractive and more sociable as a result of the project!"

BUILDINGS – THE TOWN HALL, PUBLIC TOILETS AND THE CHEESE AND GRAIN

The town hall

Over many years, the council had increasingly struggled to operate out of a completely unsuitable building near the town centre. Innumerable options for alternatives had been looked at but never happened. Then the county offered the council first option on a large building that had been the previous town hall when Frome housed a rural district council. When the rural district council was abolished in 1974, the county and district acquired the town's assets for free. It was slightly galling, therefore, to be forced to pay £250,000 to the county to take back the building for Frome.

Reclaiming the town hall evolved into a massive project. It involved significant renovation of the building but has been a great success. Taking this through to completion required a steady hand and a vast amount of work by the council; it also meant embracing the concept of borrowing money, something a more politicised council would struggle with in an era of austerity.

The town council staff occupies less than one third of the building, with the rest being a really great main meeting hall and rooms for community organisations. There've been endless hassles getting licences and agreements from the district council, but in the end the building should be largely self financing and provide a useful focal point of which the town can be really proud. This project is a classic example of IfF's capacity to take risks and go for what's right. The staff then had to work out how the money could be borrowed and the project made to stack up. The staff were massively helped in this example by Colin Cobb, one of the councillors, whose exceptional skills in helping manage the project reduced the risks considerably.

Public toilets

The provision of public toilets is a recurring theme and an incredibly important one. One expert estimates that at least a quarter of the population regularly have a pressing need to use public toilets, yet it's a subject often greeted with nervous giggles or as though it weren't worth talking about, much less making policy around.

Our district council responded to the rising costs of maintaining often vandalised toilets by simply shutting them down. The problem of keeping them open has also been exacerbated by disabled-access legislation, because many old buildings are costly, or even structurally impossible, to update. Frome Town Council's answer was to invent and put in place a scheme that funds shops and cafes to make their facilities available to all.

In another dysfunctional lack of action defying common sense, the district council's 'assets department' seemingly couldn't bear to part with the potential for profit, and this left us with six redundant buildings in a terrible state. After seven years of patient, angry, humorous and exasperated waiting, the district has finally demolished or reused them.

In parallel, but not directly linked, we've also initiated a scheme to refill water bottles using the same cafes.

The Cheese and Grain

The kickstarter for IfF was in part the community fury at the council's alleged mishandling of The Cheese and Grain (C&G), a huge 'village hall' in the middle of town. So why return to it now? My theme for 'what IfF2 has done' is consolidation and building on what we know works. This is nowhere more true than with the C&G. I would argue that the council's steady support has played a crucial role in helping the C&G become a major asset to Frome, quadrupling turnover in the last five years to £830,000 in 2017/18 and employing 50 workers.

The council co-funded a successful lottery bid in which the council's £130,000 attracted an additional £300,000 of lottery money. It has also supported one-off requests, such as converting the lighting to energy-efficient LEDs. The money borrowed was used to convert a derelict part of the building to a media centre. There is now a studio to provide facilities for musicians and bands to rehearse, record their music and capture their work on film. It will also be a location for training and the development of music and film related technical skills.

Again, the council borrowed from the Public Works Loan Board, which gives councils access to very low interest rates. In this case, the fixed rate repayment is just over £8,000 per annum until 2037. That's an extraordinarily small investment given the return to the community.

Over the last few years, since the initial renovation, the C&G has added a mass of community activities to its programme, including The Children's Festival; family roller-skating; Healthy Mondays, and all the work that goes on under this banner; a children's theatre school; adult education classes; regular free live music and so on. While all this community stuff is happening, the C&G has been able to attract serious rock bands – the Foo Fighters and Fat Boy Slim to name two.

It's a tricky balance between a publicly-owned social enterprise and a commercially-viable venue; so far the staff have done an excellent job in maintaining this.

Business strategy

The traditional role of a town council is often to focus on businesses, based on the discredited premise that wealth will filter down. Indeed, many town councillors were and still are owners and managers of businesses. A new direction, in the second IfF period, of promoting local businesses was largely due to Jean Boulton, a councillor with considerable background in this area (and another good example of where one person can really get things moving). She's worked in partnership with the economics and regeneration manager and other staff to develop a series of initiatives.

- Supporting the Frome and District Chamber of Commerce to put on networking events. Most notably these are the regular Business Breakfast and Discuss & Do.
- Promoting events that focus on what businesses need to be successful and what they can do for the town. For example, Soul Traders' events and meetings that brought together people who work alone.
- Creating The Good Business Audit, which provided access to consultants who cover areas such as economic issues, energy and environment, and social concerns. This has spawned an allied 'Good Business Award'.
- Establishing and promoting an apprenticeship scheme with the local college.

What all these activities do is build on the council's positive experiences of developing new community relationships and extend to the business community. Considerable sharing of ideas and resources between businesses has resulted, all of which moves away from a model of Victorian philanthropy, where business might dispense small sums to the poor, and towards building commitment to the common good of the town.

Frome Independent Market

Started earlier with considerable IfF support, Frome Independent Market continued to benefit from a town councillor on their board and smaller project grants. The market itself brings over 10,000 people into the town once a month and has developed as a prize-winning event that plays a key part in raising Frome's profile. The market helps generate an estimated £2.5 million a year in revenue for its traders, Frome's independent retailers and hospitality businesses.

Planning

The reformed Planning Advisory Group, supported by a full time member of staff, plays a key ongoing role. Their job is to keep an eagle eye on what both developers and the District plan to impose on Frome. Although the town may not have much power in this area, we can exert influence. There have been innumerable wins for the staff and councillors who have focussed on this aspect of civic activity, including ensuring developers actually cough up the community funds they're meant to.

Community development

Over the years there's been a steady increase in the work done to support community organisations. Essentially, this involves a member of staff constantly available to talk to and enhance the work of the mass of groups in Frome. These range from tiny groups with very little structure to those with significant staffing and resources.

There are innumerable ways in which the council staff are catalysing actions and providing inputs. Helping groups to become 'funding ready' has been key, with a service brought in by the council to provide generic training alongside tailored support for specific issues and funding applications. This has brought steady income into the town.

Alongside this, the council has continued to run a more traditional 'community grants scheme'. What has changed from earlier efforts is a considerable tightening up of criteria and more thinking about how best to support some groups with multi-year agreements. These give a degree of stability to groups the council feels are vital, like the Citizens Advice Bureau.

There's also been a more strategic approach to working with young people. For a while we experimented with a youth mayor and her deputy. Despite having excellent people in these roles, lack of connection with the community made these feel like somewhat token appointments and the roles weren't continued.

More successful was the introduction of annual youth conferences, looking to give a real experience of engagement to Frome's young people. Recently this has been linked with the People's Budget conference.

Forming a management team of staff aims to enable better linkage across different areas of work. A good example of this is community development and youth needing to relate closely to what happens in parks and open spaces. Regular meetings with the managers sitting in the same room have underpinned further improvement: now the right things are being supported in the right places. For example:
- New equipment in the main playing field and other small parks.
- An all-weather, multi-use games area.
- Significant grants to the YMCA, enabling them to carry out a whole raft of activities with young people.

- The town council continuing to link closely with Edventure: Frome, an inspirational organisation modelling a different approach to apprenticeships and youth training.

Equally, the work of the wellbeing staff has multiple overlaps with the work of the resilience manager: both centre around building a strong, informed community. An attendee at a recent youth conference wrote in:

"I've just come back from the first young people's conference at the Football Club and I have to say it was amazing. I'd urge you to pop in and see it in action from 1pm to 3pm today, when it'll be repeated with the other half of Frome's 14-year-olds.

Seeing all of the year 8s from Oakfield and Chritchill Schools completely engaged and participating in various activities from learning to scythe and designing a website was great. We heard loud and clear their priorities for Frome which were (in the main) achievable. Both sessions today finish with Selwood School performing a musical about what young people see through their eyes. Brilliant! We'll try and screen at the next Council meeting.

My congratulations to Kate Hellard and Purple Elephant for masterminding the day. And a big thank you to our Ranger team, Ruth Knagg and the ambassadors from Frome College for leading some of the activities."

Resilience

Employing a resilience officer, Anna Francis, to focus on all things environmental as well as awareness raising in relation to the state of the planet in times of austerity may, to some, seem an extravagance; FTC have found that there are many benefits – social, economic and environmental – and this work has contributed to the local success and national profile of the council.

During the second IfF period, Anna's role has focused on reducing emissions and improving resource use. Two of the notable successes are the UK's first Library of Things and the Community Fridge, ideas that have now been copied all over the UK. The Library of Things offers people the chance to borrow a wide range of items such as cooking utensils, musical instruments, gardening equipment and toys. The Community Fridge makes a real difference too: over 9,000 items (over 3 tonnes of food) pass through the fridge each month, reducing landfill as well as feeding a lot of people. That's an equivalent reduction in CO_2 of taking over 40 cars off the road for a year. The Fridge has now been augmented by a Community Larder and a Community Coat Rack, where people leave and/or take coats for free.

Transport is a massive concern in rural areas, but also increasingly so within towns as services are cut and prices rise. Without the funds, or the desire, to run bus services, FTC's approach has been to work with local campaign groups such as Bus Users to help secure local bus services and boost numbers. The council has also provided an integrated transport leaflet to all households to increase usage and awareness. We've still developed a transport strategy that embeds active and fossil-fuel free travel. As always, it's the very local that can be influenced; for example, by engaging schools through an active travel challenge car use has significantly reduced, in some areas from 70% to 30%.

At one point in Frome there were two car clubs in operation, with the council providing promotion, parking and charging for an electric vehicle. Not surprisingly, this has been reduced to one, but the one remaining car club is still a viable and popular way to access a car. In addition, the council has installed or subsidised electric car-charging points.

On the waste front, the council has worked hard to try and get business to cooperate, but again this is primarily the responsibility of the district and county. Frustratingly, we've failed to make inroads into improving reuse from the recycling centre, although there are great models of this elsewhere. When plastics hit the headlines, the council chose to work closely with community groups, providing space for meetings and some coordination while also banning single use plastics in the council's own operations.

Recognising the vital need for carbon reduction, the council commissioned research on how much energy Frome uses and how this could be decarbonised. Identifying the need to get public acceptance of this work, we focussed on 'Clean and Healthy' as the aspiration. Our initial carbon-reduction target was to be fossil free by 2046. In late 2018, after a series of 'Frome Uprising' talks, we reduced this target to carbon neutrality by 2030 and followed Bristol by declaring a Climate Emergency. Many other cities and towns have now done the same, including, usefully, both the county and district that cover Frome. The council also joined the Covenant of Mayors, the world's largest movement for local climate and energy actions, which already had nearly 10,000 signatories representing 325m inhabitants in June 2019.

This area of work is where the town budget has been significantly expanded. Over £170,000 of external grants have been raised to support resilience activities in Frome, either directly through projects or through organisations such as the Toy Library, Happy Nappy Library, Edventure, Fair Frome, Sustainable Frome, Co-Wheels, Frome Football Club and Harry's Hydro. In addition, Anna Francis co-led the campaign to save Whatcombe Fields, which raised £330,000 through community shares in 2015 and secured 13.3 hectares of land for community use. In fact £900,000 has been raised over the five years of the council's work through resilience and community projects and FRECo (Frome Renewable Energy Co-op).

Infusing sustainability throughout the work of the council comes from that mix of staff/councillor commitment and experience, rather than necessarily reflecting the position a majority of townspeople hold. The model throughout is to employ really excellent staff, with the skills and motivation to support the community to provide the inputs.

Finances and management
It's a tribute to this area of work that I almost forgot to mention it. Working away in the background, the FTC has been blessed with incredibly dedicated and skilled staff to cover these areas. At no point has there been a serious audit query, and we've never had a serious Human Resources mess up. In a world where legislation changes often and there are copious rules handed down from above, this is a remarkable achievement.

Communications
With some fantastic exceptions, looking at most town-council websites is a dreary experience. At the start of this council's tenure, we appointed a marketing and communications manager. The marketing bit is primarily to make sure the town hall is used for events and is full of tenants. The communications bit recognises the importance of letting people know what the council is up to; this has expanded into sharing with people what everyone else in the town is up to too. At the core of our communication strategy are two linked websites: one is targeted at visitors and potential businesses and the other towards residents. Every month there are now hundreds of thousands of unique visitors to the website from within and outside of Frome.

The communication manager has now recruited a team of three, including an apprentice. There's now capacity to run things like the Breaking the Mould Conference and to maintain a website that's fast becoming the 'go to place' for what's on in Frome. The team also regularly inputs into Facebook, Twitter and Instagram. They manage one-off events, such as supporting people who were affected by a large fire by coordinating donations, and of course share information. Now all this is in place, it is hard to see how the council could ever have done without it.

DID EVERYTHING WORK THEN?
In my view, one of the things that's been less successful is our analysis of what didn't work; we've been good at admitting to our mistakes but not so good at learning from them. The things that didn't go to plan fall into two areas: larger strategic decisions

and individual projects. To repeat, it's hard to separate IfF and the council from these failures; as the staff were only carrying out instructions, it's probably fair for IfF to take the blame.

Larger strategic decisions

I've already covered IfF and the council's relationships with the district and (to a lesser extent) the county. While the conflicts have meant some things didn't happen or were slower to happen, I'm proud to have retained most of our principles.

Should we have spent so much time and money on the Neighbourhood Plan, much of it in the earlier IfF council? Probably not. However, my disappointment isn't universally shared and maybe the Neighbourhood Plan will prove more useful in times to come.

Should we have started down the route of trying to remodel the town centre? If we'd known how obstructionist and dysfunctional the district council was at the start, I doubt we'd have gone there. I'm delighted the remodeling has gotten to where it has, but very disappointed it's not better. On balance, I think it would've been a better use of energy and funds to concentrate on the things we had full control over.

Two linked accusations are often raised against the council. Firstly, that we've failed to recognise the needs of the people who've always lived here. And secondly, that in presiding over the gentrification of Frome, we're responsible for increased house prices and other perceived negative changes. Are these fair criticisms? Are we just 'blow ins' from London taking over the town? After 30 years of living and working here, I feel this is as much my home as those whose families have been here forever. The councillors are the people who've stepped up, anyone can, and IfF has consistently targeted a wide range of backgrounds. In 2015, roughly half or the IfF councillors were born in Frome.

Yes, Frome has changed, much of it for the better. Our response to the housing and accommodation crisis has been to support Fair Housing for Frome. There are no easy answers to these kinds of problems, but staying as we were was not a sensible option if Frome was to have both cheap housing and a thriving economy to provide work.

Projects that never took off

One of the attempts to help with housing needs is expressed in the Neighbourhood Plan, which called for increased opportunities for self-build. The council spent a lot of time (and some money) perusing an option to buy land that would've enabled significant self-build. Eventually, this floundered when we realised road access was insufficient. With greater experience, we might've got out earlier or never started this project.

I feel a slight pang of guilt remembering my plea to fellow councillors to persuade them to commit yet further funds for a database system that was never completed. Retrospectively, they should've stopped me. I was blinded by a desire to have an accessible list of who does what in Frome. There are funds for one in 2020, so it'll be the next council who presides over its success or continued failure.

Another thing that never took off was our bespoke Frome crowd-funding platform for local groups. In the end we abandoned it as was just too difficult to support groups to prepare their case for funding.

Our attempt to create an in-house Volunteer Bureau also floundered. There still seems to be a need for a 'dating agency' between those who want to volunteer and the positions available, but again, it never took off.

Sometimes there have simply been too many things that aren't the highest priority and they drop off the list. I'm sure the technical hitches that prevent live streaming of meetings could be overcome; we've failed to find a way to deal with unsightly street advertising or to renovate the town's unique streetlamps; we've not yet managed to produce useful guidance on street furniture. We would've been able to plant more trees in public spaces had the district not stopped every move to do so, but we've failed to find ways around this. I suspect if one councillor had really championed trees, the problem would have been cracked.

So ultimately much of this list comes down to things that the district stopped us doing and which we might have achieved with a better district-council relationship. There were those ideas that dropped off the radar because we were trying to achieve too much, and there were those ideas that were tried but failed. In the end, though, it's important to remember that these were just small mistakes; no one died.

Taxing the people

So, surely all this activity has resulted in eye-watering local tax increases, further squeezing the poor in times of austerity? Surprisingly, it hasn't. During my period as a town councillor there's never been a limit on the local tax rate we could set. This is unlike the higher levels, which are restricted by central government edicts. All the work of the council has been achieved with an average budget (from 2011 - 2019) of just over £1m. While IfF raised the local precept by 20% in 2012 and 10% in 2016 (i.e. following the elections), the average rise has been 6%, which equates to around £7 a year for a better-off household. There was incredibly little protest at any point, and given the scale of the town's ambition and what has been achieved, this relatively small increase seems a remarkable achievement.

6. Relationships with other councils

Sketch by Cllr Stina Falle – Green Party Cllr Shane Collins talks to Mendip District Council on Climate Change

Relationship with Mendip District Council

When asked about our greatest failure as IfF, I usually cite our relationship with the District Council (Mendip). This doesn't mean I accept the blame for the dysfunctional relationship that has largely existed between us, nor does it mean I can see how we could have done things better. We are clearly not alone in this struggle with the next tier of local government. Over the years I have spoken to many, many others deeply frustrated by the level of local government above them.

Some of the problems arise because of lack of resources; austerity has stripped out the District's funding by central government so much so that they are unable to function effectively. A senior staff member once described their only priority as 'financial survival'. Our failure was much greater than this though.

For the year I acted as Leader of the Council, when we wanted to develop something of a more constructive and supportive relationship with Mendip we failed. After a couple of appallingly condescending meetings I slipped back, beaten, to Frome. The problem, as I see it, is that the then Conservative cabinet in the District Council had absolute power. Many of the individuals in those posts had been there for years and they have never understood IfF as anything other than 'opposition'. I believe our success has been deeply painful to them, apparently resulting in a policy of 'lose lose is better than Frome getting anything'. Frome has 25% of the district's population but has rarely been visited by any senior Mendip councillors or staff, or received anything but hassle from them.

A further example comes from Frome councillor Mark Dorrington's feedback on his presentation to the District on carparking charges: *"Tonight I had the pleasure of presenting our petition, signed by 6179 people, against Sunday car parking charges to Mendip District Council's (MDC) Full Council. I was allowed five minutes to talk, within 15 minutes of debate. This was described as 'rabble rousing' before the official response of '£2 is nothing', one Mendip councillor even getting two one pound coins out of his pocket for dramatic effect... Not a great night and I felt like I was being told off by the headmaster. "*

As mentioned earlier, austerity has savaged local authorities' budgets, but it's a toxic mix when this is lathered in Party. Frome has had some of its ambitions severely curtailed because the district holds the planning powers as well as still owning assets in town. Their attempts to capitalise on these assets has invariably added to cynicism about councils.

There needs to be clarity as to why higher level councils are divesting themselves of their assets and asking lower levels to take on services. A fellow parish councillor puts it well: *"The County came to us and said, take these services on, or they will stop. Simple as that; no commitment to devolution just saying to us, if you want these things, you pay. That's not devolution, that's blackmail and it's not because the county has had a conversion to the virtues of parish councils, it's because it's run out of money and can't do things itself any more."*

There has been an inherent unfairness in the disposal of assets. Historically the district and county levels of an authority would have acquired assets from parish and town councils in order to manage them efficiently. However now the town's tax-payers are being forced to buy back those same assets. To add insult to injury the acquisition comes with the additional burden of legal fees. Within this, it's been the abuse of power that has been the most galling. Endless condescending conversations in which it is made quite clear who is giving and who might receive if they behave.

After we'd tried everything we could think of, ifF has essentially encouraged the staff to develop good working relationships and tried to avoid provoking the dinosaur in its death throes. We've also made every effort to develop relationships 'sideways' avoiding the district and county and linking to bodies like the NHS, while retaining a key focus on the community of Frome, where we can make changes without endless hindrance.

To add two things to this general rant. Firstly, the stance taken by the District has added considerably to the workload of Frome Town Council staff. Not only is it tedious to try and tiptoe through the relationship, but frequently town staff have had to do the work of others, as well as endlessly requesting things to be done.

In addition, there have been key areas where work has been created totally unnecessarily. The most obvious of these related to our longstanding desire to change the focus of priority in the town centre from the car to the people. Central to this has been removing a small number of parking spaces, which backed out into the main road on a dangerous corner right in the middle of Frome.

The Town Council decided that if the area belonged to Frome they could use it to create some public space. They would even pay for all the changes themselves. However two enormous hurdles stood in our way. The District not only owned the land, but had it in their power to grant planning consent, or not.

While they agreed to our spending money improving their land, in what appeared to me, rightly or wrongly, to be an act of political revenge for the IfF electoral victory, planning permission was rejected. We appealed and a year later the three relevant applications were all granted in the Town's favour with costs awarded to Frome. The staff time and cost of all this is ridiculous, never mind the frustration.

Secondly my biggest surprise as a councillor and one of my greatest disappointments has been the ways in which people elected at various levels, to serve their communities, have failed to work together and have put their petty party politics first. For the staff, at all levels, having to deal with this must be deeply exasperating. In the 2019 elections, two thirds of the Conservative District councillors lost their seats, including the Leader. One can only hope this makes a significant difference, though the majority Lib Dems decision to cobble together an alliance with various non IfF style independents, rather than the large collection of Greens, does not bode well.

As so often, it is the underlying system that is totally unsuited to the 21st century. Without sufficient resources, or meaningful contact with the community, the District Council as an entity is doomed. Before too long it is inevitable that this middle level of local government will be dissolved. The question then for Frome will then be whether resources and power move even further from the town, or can they be returned here.

Supporting other councils – 'Breaking the Mould'

There is a 'National Association of Local Councils' (NALC) with affiliated organisations in each county. They represent the interests of local councils. While Frome's Town Clerk apparently values the support he gets for the town's annual subscription, I have never benefitted in any tangible way from their 'representation of the interests of 80,000 councillors'. My only contact with them has led me to view the Association as part of the system that ensures the maintenance of the status quo. Certainly, there has never been a pro-active approach from them to share and disseminate ideas between councils at a town level.

Both as councillors and staff we'd been approached many times, by parishes and towns around the country to network ideas. Mel Usher proposed a conference aimed at councillors and senior staff of the larger town councils which led to one of our most effective projects, the Breaking the Mould conference. In April 2018 Frome council hosted a special one-day event for councillors and staff to come together to immerse themselves in key topics.

The conference had the aim of catalysing new ways to share good practice beyond Town Clerks' meetings and the limite d NALC efforts. The day took the format of interactive workshops, discussion panels, informal get togethers and learning opportunities. Videos and follow up on key areas are still available on the Frome Town Council website.

There was really excellent feedback from many of those who attended and enjoyed Frome council's spirit of not being selfish with our experiences or resources. Having said that, there has not been much follow up and the planned evening fringe event didn't become the hotbed of discussion I'd hoped, though the Rye Bakery pizza was excellent. However we should not have to depend on the Fromes of this world to organise and fund this process. Ultimately, unless the official support structures, like NALC, recognise the need to build a more effective layer of local government, and unless there is funding for this, good practice will never be shared and built on. A further layer of ad hoc informal support and exchange has come via the *Flatpack Democracy* website and Facebook Forum for Independent Councillors.

Pam Barrett, the leading light in Buckfastleigh's revolution, and I, manage the Forum where around 170 new councillors and aspiring candidates share ideas. This was especially lively leading up to the 2019 elections and then to bolster the courage of new councillors in taking on the old guard and, where necessary, the clerks. We have also run live video conferences and continue to spend time with new councils with the same aim.

This is, however, unsustainable in time and energy, re-emphasising the point that as central government has presided over the destruction of local services, it should take responsibility for building the capacity of local communities to do stuff for themselves. Free copies of *Flatpacks 1* and *2.0* to the 100,000 parish councillors would be a good start.

7. What happened elsewhere

These are among the groups of Independents standing in local elections on May 2nd 2019. They reject the farce of Party politics in favour of reclaiming politics for the people.

Introduction

My original aim in writing *Flatpack Democracy* was for the book to act as a catalyst and to provoke experimentation in the democratic model. I hoped that other models would evolve and improve on our initial democratic adventures. We've sold over 5,000 copies and sent some to unlikely places like Finland and New Zealand. On reflection, maybe that's not so surprising given that almost everywhere power has been hijacked from the communities the politicians purport to serve.

Frome is not unique; around the UK there are many great initiatives and some really effective councillors and councils. There are innumerable pilots, projects and associated reports and academic studies you can immerse yourself in to gain a wider picture of the potential.

Over the last five years I've been in touch with numerous people trying to change their local council, and I've spoken at a great many meetings. I have a list of places where some really interesting action is taking place, which currently has around 120 councils on it.

I followed just over 50 of these groups as they prepared for the May 2019 elections. As a result, I know of 19 places (including ACT for Cuxton Together, Whitehill & Bordon Community Party, Ecclesfield Independents and Minehead) who face the welcome challenge of working with nothing but independents. Portishead, who'd run such a long and energetic campaign, were rewarded with 12/14 seats. Hadleigh Together, who emerged from the playground a few months before the election won 13/15 seats. A whole group in Devon, with close links in support and energy to Buckfastleigh, who already had four year's experience of radical rule, have emerged.

Another 16 on my list are headed 'key independents elected'. These include councillors in Bournemouth/Christchurch/Poole, Shepton Mallet, Wells, Didcot, and others who will have various degrees of struggle and success in trying to change the system.

Another group is headed 'no significant success', where it looks like individual councillors will struggle to impose themselves (and I hope I am proven wrong and they can do so). More than half of these are at district, county or unitary authority levels.

There's also a final group who I know nothing about. They are places from where every now and then a new councillor gets in touch with their story, having bought *Flatpack Democracy* and entered the fray.

However, what I've set out to do here is provide examples, with some direct quotes, of the ways some of Frome's political ideas have been used and some lessons that can be drawn. This chapter is based primarily on a dozen detailed conversations my colleague Peter Andrews has had with key individuals in other independent councils, following up on what we already knew about their work. We also drew on postings and conversations from the 170 new councillors in the Independents' Facebook Group.

The three criteria for inclusion in this chapter about independents elsewhere were:
- That the councillors are working outside of national party politics and the systems and traditions of national politics. While most councillors at parish and town level will claim to be independents, most of them operate in the hierarchical and confrontational way of national politics. Larger places still tend to elect their councillors based on their party political membership. However,

I'm only interested here in genuine independence from the national party ideologies and a focus on local policies and engagement

- Closely linked to the first criterion (and borne out by our own research) is that to be effective members need to share some form of agreed Ways of Working
- That the councillors are inter ested in more than simply moving party politics to one side, in addition to recognising the paramount necessity for translating ambition to achievement at a truly local level.

Why do it?

So why, in the last few years, have a completely new set of people put themselves forward for election as councillors? Primarily there is a desperation with the status quo which drives many people to try to do things better. The system, from top to bottom, is manifestly undemocratic, and when overlaid with the effects of austerity has created a toxic mix that many people at a local level are desperate to do something about. If there was a need for us to create an IfF in 2011, that need is far greater now.

Personally, I've always been attached to the idea of 'local and global'. In other words, aiming to join small local changes together to build a mass movement for fundamental change. Change from the bottom up. While this motivates some of those I spend time with, for the majority the purely 'local' takes priority. Recognising that there's potential for change at this level is what has inspired most people to enter the game.

They start to see what Jason Leman summarises well in his MSc on municipalism:
"… local councils can help create virtuous spirals. They can help solve local problems through connecting and supporting local groups and individuals, providing spaces to talk and think about solutions, and gathering or mobilising resources to act. Being relatively small and embedded in the local area, local councils are better able to respond to local problems and innovate to find solutions than larger public bodies."

Historically, parish and town councils were basically fine just keeping an eye on the park and commenting on planning applications. Not any longer. Add to this a growing awareness that 'if we don't do it, no one else will', and you can see why people are prepared to get involved.

Politics without realising it

Our final three candidates are three Hadleigh Dads who co-founded Hadleigh Together after talking about local issues on the school run and dreaming up a better way of doing things…

Hadleigh Together, who won 13/15 seats in May 2019.

Many of those who took part in the 2019 elections had never imagined they would stand for office; it certainly hadn't been in their plans a few months before! In many cases, an unpleasant incident with the local council or long period of council inaction had frustrated them into standing. In an increasing number of places desire for action has come directly from voluntary and community groups. They've become aware of how they might be supported by a functioning council, or at least not obstructed by an ineffective one. Those standing also then realised that to create change they'd need to work together with others as a group of independents.

It took me a few years to realise I'd become a politician. Most people entering local politics start off by being fairly horrified by the prospect: in most people's minds politics is associated with the widely discredited political parties. A Welsh independent councillor I spoke with said: *"For a lot of us our community comes before our political view, so being an independent is our only real choice."*

She's right. It is hard to properly represent the community and follow a predetermined party line. It's this that brings many community activists into independent politics.

Coming from the community has two vital advantages: firstly, you're likely to understand key concerns; secondly, you come with a set of people likely to be initial supporters or have access to such a group.

The following extracts come from interviews with parties that grew out of community action: *"All of the core group are involved in community activity. We are planning a series of meetings and networking events that are based around community groups. People respond to people not adverts, which attract all the 'usual suspects' whereas social networks can get to people not normally associated with politics. Personal connections will have a far higher success rate in terms of converting people to the cause than almost any other method."*

Future Shepton

"I got involved in local politics because of my local playground. I don't mind where you stand on this issue, the fact is when I went to the town council I was defeated. Not, I think, because of what I was saying in particular, but because of the way I was going about it. In retrospect perhaps I should have joined the Conservative party and started bribing the public with M&S vouchers in the time-honoured tradition, to get my way.

"Instead, first of all, I went to them. Big mistake! No one from the public ever goes to town council meetings, what was I doing there? A few councillors even deigned to look around at me, a member of the public, in the public gallery!

"Second, I told them – politely – that they might have made the wrong decision. And I asked them to look again at it. Mistake number two: they never makes a bad decision, especially seeing as it's usually a white male of a certain age (or prematurely aged) proposing the motion, and we have to agree they never get anything wrong. Especially what with them being experts in playgrounds.

"I got nowhere. The room wasn't set up for listening. It was set up for lots of other things: deference, defensiveness, ceremony, secrecy... but it didn't want to deal with a member of the public. I have never felt more unwelcome."

Indy Monmouth candidate

'Inspired' (or perhaps 'enraged') by this experience, the writer initiated the independent group the Indy Monmouth. Not elected herself the first time, she stood in a by-election and was defeated by two votes (it would have been one, but her husband forgot to vote). At the next by-election, she emerged victorious and is now a member of the largest group on the council.

In Haswell Community in County Durham, the successful independent movement was initiated by someone who '... had applied to be co-opted onto the council six times but had received no reply at all from the existing councillors...' The group went on to win every seat.

The Essentials: have they been essential for others?

In *Flatpack Democracy* I set out five things I felt were essential for an independent group to take power. They were:
   1) Work as a group
   2) Agree your Ways of Working
   3) Use a facilitator
   4) Keep it light
   5) Get all the help you can

So what has been the experience of others in relation to these, not just in the initial stages but later, if they were elected?

Work as a group

There's absolute clarity from all those we spoke to that this is essential. 'Don't try and do it alone' and 'You need the support of like-minded people who want to stand' were just two of the comments we received.

In bigger places, or where there is a history of strong party politics, working as a group makes election possible. Together the process can be really enjoyable instead of the massive battle faced by individuals acting alone.

As well as practical tasks like delivering leaflets, there's the experience of working with others to create a campaign and the benefits of sharing and testing ideas. Where candidates have been elected, working closely together is clearly linked to ambition and achievement. There are many councils full of individuals each doing their own thing, the evidence I find is that they achieve much less.

There are places where the independents set out as a group but fragmented or disbanded after getting elected. Again, from those we've talked to, this fragmentation results in fewer enterprising achievements, which neatly brings me to the Ways of Working.

Agree your Ways of Working

I've commented earlier on how IfF did (and did not) use our Ways of Working to the group's advantage. Their initial value comes in at the selection stage by drawing some boundaries to help form the selection criteria. Indeed, this is the only boundary. If there's no recognition from the members as to how the group will work together or agreed underpinning values, anyone can be part of the group – and in that case why be a group? There were a number of places where the absence of agreed values allowed people into a group who later caused considerable disruption and upset.

During the election campaign, Ways of Working have been important for many groups: agreed common ground on behaviour and the broad direction of travel make it possible for relative strangers to work in harmony. This gives the members the confidence to disagree without the normal paradigms of conflict, revenge, anger and so on.

Where candidates (and then councillors) have come from one specific area of their society, they'll find it easier to work as a group. This was the case for Future Shepton, for example, whose candidates were mainly community workers. The disadvantage of this is that it reduces the range of the community represented and the ideas they would bring with them. Personally, I believe it's very important that in all cases a strong and mutually-agreed Ways of Working is quickly established. Then there'll be a way to enable differences of opinion to become a positive rather than a destructive factor.

Different Ways of Working

Frome's initial Ways of Working, along with the core values of The Alternativet party in Denmark, seem to have been a useful starting point for others. Encouragingly, groups have then added, removed and adjusted to suit their own situation. Amongst those groups we've looked at there's a whole range of mechanisms, from cases where candidates formally sign up to a set of values through to an informal expectation that councillors behave as they would like to see others do in everyday life – a case of 'do as you would be done by'. This may be complemented by election pledges to, for example 'be open about everything we do'.

There's much common ground in the Ways of Working different groups have come up with, here are a small selection:
- Our debates are rational, courteous, to the point and lead to a conclusion
- We see admitting mistakes or having our minds changed as positive
- We trust and respect other people's knowledge, expertise and experience
- We believe if we are having fun doing it, it'll turn out better than we ever hoped
- Listen attentively – one person speaking at any time
- Be open minded and prepared to change your mind
- Question evidence, information, assumptions
- Sustain an intention to involve each other and others, rather than work in isolation
- Be honest and transparent – give reasons for decisions
- Be inclusive and respectful of differences – avoid being personal
- Be constructive, solution focused and forward thinking
- Be creative and use others' skills/ideas to do stuff differently and better
- Ensure that the council acts as a bridge and facilitator for our community
- Offer community leadership and be answerable to residents and not a political party
- Be a convener who will facilitate open, honest and unrushed conversations
- Support good ideas and take practical action regardless of the party affiliation of those sponsoring them.
- Be inclusive and respectful of differences and seek to develop empathy for different viewpoints
- Be creative and use others' skills and ideas to do stuff differently and better.

This list could do with some academic follow up and sorting into the 'vision values' and 'humanity values' that Emil Husted investigates in his study of Alternativet's work. He helpfully separates points into deep values and debating principles, making the case that as long as enough of each is agreed, things can hold together. We should not pretend that 'horizontal' organisations, with minimal leadership or formal membership, without holding votes or having a rulebook, are easy to maintain. A skeleton of core values and agreement on process seems to be essential.

As we found in Frome, to be really effective also requires effort to make sure members are supported and encouraged to adopt and hold these ideals. In other words, Ways of Working take work! They need regular attention. It is not simply enough to create them and then leave them in some forgotten folder.

What happens without Ways of Working?

There were a number of groups we spoke to who regretted not having spent time developing formal, or even informal, Ways of Working. These regrets fall into three areas:

- That the process would have brought the group together.
- That Ways of Working would have made it easier to address friction when it occurred.
- That there would've been greater collective ambitions.

Having said this, I reiterate that there really is no right answer. A light touch has worked well for some groups (mainly in smaller communities) with 'how they work together' emerging informally.

A number of groups, who started off in broadly similar ways to Frome but lacked agreed values have not produced significantly different outcomes from the councils they replaced. Others without these agreements have collapsed impressively after elections (whether in power or opposition). This in part comes down to the fact that the concept of independents working together hadn't been worked through, so there were differing views of what an independent was and how they should behave.

Some wanted to meet together as a group; some thought an independent should be completely independent and plough their own furrow politically. They struggled with the idea of being able to disagree and yet be part of a cohesive group. The use of outside facilitators for support might have prevented these struggles.

Use a facilitator

The feedback on using facilitation is that it's an incredibly important part of the group process, especially at the start. Almost inevitably, without the use of a facilitator, the person who takes on the role of chair and the more dominant characters in the group will begin to assume the leading roles, usually to the detriment of the group as a whole. It's hard to see how real changes in the way things are done can evolve, when the model we know tends to be perpetuated.

Many groups have found it a challenge to find someone who works with groups as a profession and will work at little or no cost. In Frome we've been incredibly lucky to attract people whose contribution to IfF has been their time in facilitation. It may be possible to find the kind of person who would be called an 'elder' in other societies, people able to command respect while guiding the group impartially.

In most cases, after initial use of facilitation, the groups we've spoken to have decided to go it alone. This has both been successful and unsuccessful. However, several groups have had great results when they've reintroduced facilitation back into their process for specific meetings.

Early and important decisions are particularly vulnerable to poor process because as well as making the decision there's lots going on in terms of power and group dynamics. Where groups decide by voting alone, it's important to remember that there will always be winners and losers.

The example below from Torridge Common Ground shows what can happen without facilitation; had the group held a facilitated discussion, they might not have ended up in a messy situation likely to take a long time to recover from.

"Last week we had about 15 members at a meeting, not the previous turnout of about 40–50 people. One of the groups within the 15 members decided that they would prefer to change the group name, as they believed that they could reach out to the community easier with this name. Hands went up and the vote went with the change; therefore, at that moment we are changing names again. On reflection I believe we made a fundamental blunder right at the start of our journey, the 15 members were an extreme minority based on our actual group size of 50+ people, the reality of that vote is that about eight out of our 50 members won a vote only because there were only 15 of us there that night. We could be back and forth on issues like name changes each month and the only thing defining who wins the vote will be who brings the most friends."

As one contact put it: *"In the early years it was not so much a problem of 'consultation fatigue' as 'confrontation fatigue'."*

Keep it light

Talking to a group in Dorchester, one of them mentioned how much fun he was having. We don't associate politics with fun, but I believe strongly that to attract a range of people who will stay the course, things have to be kept light; that view is widely shared by those we spoke to.

The best councillors often turn out to be busy people with many alternative ways to spend their time. This means to attract them the whole process of being a councillor should be enjoyable, not simply having endless dry meetings then going to the pub later. There's a certain type of person who specialises in rules, regulations, agendas and the minutiae of meetings; this sort of man – and it is usually a man – can strangle the life and creativity from a group if he's not carefully managed.

Incidentally, the pub is not a comfortable place for some people and it's really important not to build exclusion into these social moments. For this reason, IfF 2019 has broken with earlier habits by not following meetings with the pub, which strikes me as a good decision as long as they find other ways to build relationships outside council meetings. Early facilitation can ensure that there are enjoyable and light ways to build relationships, and groups that have done so have found their revolutions easier, more productive and generally enjoyable.

Get all the help you can

It may seem obvious, but it's essential. Groups that have found ways to draw in practical help have found the whole election process much easier. From leaflet delivery to raising funds or keeping the Facebook page up-to-date, the wider the active supporter-base the better. I've noticed that groups that have their origins in community groups find this more natural than individuals who come with an ideology of independence but not the community contacts.

Ambition

One of my aims in writing this chapter is to dispel the thought that 'it's only Frome'. In talking to other groups, there often emerged a real pride in what has been achieved where a majority independent group have developed Ways of Working and an ambitious approach. Below are a few quotes from these groups – they only touch the surface of what has changed.

"Am I proud? More than doubling turnout across both wards in the 2017 election – to 56%, one of the highest in the UK."

"Dom re-codified the standing orders by dividing them up into more relevant sections, stripping out irrelevant material, and making sure that what was said to be statutory actually was. They have done away with the three minute rule, whereby a member of the public can speak to a

motion, during the debate of that motion, for only three minutes. They have substituted this with a 30 minute open session at the beginning of the council sessions where anyone can speak for five minutes or even longer, if necessary, on a topic that is vexing them."

"We now have a well functioning, well used website."

"Before the council never had aims and objectives – now we have them for all to see on their website and the priorities are translated into action."

"The town council now works with a range of other organisations in the area. Although it has a small budget, it is in an ideal position to influence and act as a catalyst."

"We now have a community magazine, with open communication: the more you celebrate the more people get involved."

"Incomers and businesses speak positively about the town as a place that has potential."

"We had nine Conservative councillors before they were all replaced, in 2015, with independents. Quite a lot has happened since then: we have built a new medical centre and completed a renovation of the Festival Hall; we have also set up a Youth Council and encouraged the growth or development of a number of community organisations (at the last Annual Parish Meeting of the old Parish Council, no community groups were present, this year there were 14); various fundraising efforts have been undertaken, for example the staging at the Festival Hall, a planter appeal and most recently, the 'there but not there' Tommy appeal; we have also launched a Neighbourhood Plan and will be running a community consultation on our initial draft policies very shortly; all the time, we have been very careful to keep residents up to date with what we are doing on their behalf, notably through the introduction of a quarterly newsletter. We all feel that the last three and a half years have been a big success story and we are aiming to retain our seats at the next elections in May 2019."

"We have been able to enact real change in our town since the election of 10 out of 12 independent councillors. Councillors have now settled into a new way of working together. In addition, the council has reduced the amount of time spent on non-productive activities. They no longer go out to meet businesses and organisations, who instead come in to the council, while larger organisations are now consultees. The council has also changed their grant process with more formal applications, encouraging more members of the public to apply. We are working with councillors to ensure that grants are in line with council strategy and have instituted a follow up process. The council's work has also included a new youth strategy, revitalised business strategy and tourism development. It is also now seeking to achieve dementia friendly status."

Deciding what's possible: standing at district, county and unitary authority levels levels

Can the concept of a values-led group be taken to higher tiers of local government? This is the question I have been asked most over the last few years. In part, this is in recognition of the limited powers there are at a town or parish level and a hankering for some real action.

At one stage, IfF registered as a major political party that could stand at the next level up so that we could compete at district level. After careful research, we felt it would be just about impossible to take power because too many seats are in rural areas, held by long-standing incumbents with vast majorities. Power could only be gained through coalitions, but this is especially tricky when your model is radically different and there's no membership or manifesto to work with in negotiations.

For others, the maths or the ambition is different, and in a number of places new groups have registered as parties and stood. Until 2019, none I know of gained significant numbers of seats. In competition with the national political parties, it's probably essential to have something closer to a manifesto (see Local Parties below), which implies forming as early as possible in order to create and agree a manifesto with candidates and membership.

Having advised potential candidates not to stand above town/parish levels, I was proven at least partially wrong in 2019.

The Alliance for Local Living (ALL) in Dorset won seats at the town level but also in the new unitary authority Bournemouth/Christchurch/Poole (BCP) level. Felicity Rice, one of the founders of ALL, takes up their story: *"So, now we have two members of indies in the cabinet in BCP – Andy Hadley for transport, and myself for environment and climate change AND there are six independents in the cabinet of 10 AND an independent chair of the council (of 76) AND 19 independents (out of 76) :) Whoahey!"*

ALL BCP clearly see themselves looking to introduce ideas of greater informality and new ways of running the council, working from within the coalition, and given the size of their presence, have a real opportunity to do so. What they have achieved is even more remarkable when one hears stories from elsewhere.

In East Devon 45 years of Conservative rule came to an end with an 'Independent Group' leading a minority administration. That sounds good until a closer look reveals there was potential for a few of the new group to have allied with 11 of the previously established East Devon Independent Alliance (EDIA). Instead, the individual 'independents' revealed themselves as ex-Tories, and by bringing members of the previous Tory administration into key committee positions have orchestrated a textbook counter revolution, remaining in power despite their losses and independent gains.

It turns out that while over 14% of councillors were elected as independents in the 2019 local elections at district level, many were 'independents' in name only. During campaigns, in trying to form coalitions, and even when in power, new independents often seem to face intense opposition, primarily I believe because the establishment finds change so hard to contemplate and deal with.

Bath and North East Somerset Independent Group (BIG) are a great example of where there was an attempt to really rock the boat at a unitary authority level . BIG offered a radical non-party model with Ways of Working and a promise of real change to a participatory democracy. In the end BIG failed to gain enough support and didn't come close to gaining any seats.

Bath & North East Somerset (B&NES) has, since the dawn of time, see-sawed between LibDem and Tory control. The Tory incumbents hadn't been a successful or progressive council, overlay that with the toxic Brexit debate and the 'anything but the Tories' syndrome kicked in. If you couple that with the sheer amount of resources thrown at the area by the LibDems – some residents received over 20 leaflets and several door knockings – it was always going to be an uphill task.

Another factor was that BIG was only formed as a group a year and a half before the election. This ultimately meant there wasn't enough time to find sufficient candidates or for them to get their message across to the community before election day. Where BIG did stand, their message was well received, garnering a very respectable number of votes, beating Labour in seven out of 10 wards. However, the publicity needed to overcome the party machines and the extent to which the political parties came together to oppose BIG provided an invaluable learning so they can start on a much stronger footing for the 2023 elections.

The Belgian groups which failed to get elected put this down to a 'ganging up' by the politicians to ensure that power remained with them. Post election this can be true too. In Didcot, for example, the seven new independents were completely sidelined by the nine-member Labour group supported by two Conservatives. They combined to vote in a Labour council leader and Conservative mayor and they also denied the independents any representation on the key committees.

After these depressing tales, it's worth noting that there are clearly individuals making a difference on district and county councils, like Craig Browne who is a parish councillor with Alderly Edge First; Cheshire East's deputy leader in Conservative heartlands; and Gavin Gwilym, the Cynon Valley Party's sole representative in Labour's birthplace of Rhondda Cynon Taf.

I started this section by stating that the 2019 elections showed I was at least partially wrong to advise people not to compete at higher levels in 2019. I do think it's impossible to take on the party system and win, but the battle itself may well be worth fighting if only because of the change it leads to. There's also some evidence that incursions into coalitions can potentially show it is worth doing, and if individuals have the energy to battle away, they can make a change. It does, however, require an element of luck to arrive at a situation where independents have significant influence. I stick to my view that what we've experimented with in Frome is most relevant at local levels.

And at a national level?

I'm also often asked about values led politics at a national level. Based on the analysis above in relation to the UK, it'll be no surprise that my response is that this will never happen.

I come back to the Danish Alternativet party, who had an initial 'manifestoless' approach. Considering it was a brand new party and working in a proportional representation system, they achieved the Holy Grail, with 10 MPs as well as mayors and councillors at lower levels. In most European countries, there are almost always coalitions, no one party holds outright power. The Alternativet has played a really important role in poking the system and introducing new ideas as a floating member of coalitions.

However, once in parliament they morphed into something much more like a party than a movement, losing some of their really radical ideas. This will have contributed to the 2019 election results in which they lost all but four seats. However, the successful parties attributed some of their new environmental and climate change focus to Alternativet as all but the far right parties massively upped their proposals in these areas. My conclusion of this is that Alternativet did manage to do something truly remarkable in their initial term but lost their way by being absorbed into 'The System'. As time has gone on their radical and 'different from the others' stance has changed, and they've started to look like a traditional party. It's unclear if they will survive at all, but their Green legacy will.

Create your own community council through the Localism Act

To my surprise, only around 25% of the population live in communities served by parish and town councils and their Scottish and Welsh equivalents. The rest have even less potential for contact with their representatives, a situation exacerbated where there are only cities and less populated rural areas. Witness the fact that Scotland has the worst democractic representation per head in Europe (followed by Denmark).

The Localism Act of 2011 includes the provision to create a new parish or community council. All it takes is 7.5% of local electors to sign a petition asking for a new council and then... it usually all goes wrong: there's a massive flaw in the Localism Act that's impacted on many of Frome's ambitions and does so here too. The 'principal authority', i.e. the layer of council above, can trump (I'm trying to reclaim the word) the wishes of the people. They make the final choice.

So, for example, although 9,000 people took part in consultations in Bexhill, with 93.5% supporting the creation of a new town council, Rother District Council had other ideas. They cited the 'silent majority that hadn't voted' because they were 'happy with the status quo' and described the move as a 'Momentum plot' in rejecting the application. Bexhill still doesn't have a council, but inspiringly 13 independents stood in the 2019 district elections as Bexhill Town Council and after all being elected are now part of the ruling Rother Alliance.

Other examples

David Gee of Bexhill in Rother District, East Sussex said: *"We had a lot of support from the community for a new parish. We'd put out a survey, collected the responses and it was obvious people wanted a parish council. We asked for a local referendum, but the district wouldn't call one. Then the district did its own consultation and said there wasn't enough support and it went to a vote at the council and was lost. We knew the council leader and our local councillor didn't want a parish and they stopped it."*

So, although the National Association of Local Councils heralded a 'new wave of councils' in 2015, the initial seven have only been joined by a further seven four years later. What's more, those four include the reinstatement of Shrewsbury and Salisbury town councils after they lost them in earlier local government reorganisations.

Amongst the wreckage are two examples I want to pick up on. In Sutton Coldfield, in the suburbs of Birmingham, community members put in hours of time and effort over a three-year period to achieve a new town council only to see party politicians emerge at the last moment to take most of the seats. Birmingham is currently consulting on whether to expand the number of parish councils beyond the current two.

The other example I'd like to look at is Queen's Park, until recently London's only community council and the first to be formed for 80 years. This emerged in 2012 after a decade of solid community-development work, with most of the new councillors co-opted. After an initially challenging period, primarily because of lack of experience and virtually non-existent support from the city council, they seem to be playing an increasingly important role. Without this level of local government, meeting your representative in cities means engaging with a vast machine of bureaucracy and distant politicians.

In the Queen's Park case, the council has been sufficiently ignored for the political parties to stay away. A second community council in London is now in the stage of 'community governance review'.

Variants on the *Flatpack* model

I've frequently stressed that we didn't set out to create a Frome or even a *Flatpack* model that should be rigidly adhered to. There are significantly different approaches to dealing with the same challenges we faced in Frome. Below are some I have engaged with over the last few years:

The anti political party party

In a number of places independents have stood together simply to get rid of the parties. For example a group from North Cornwall said: *"We need a town council composed of elected members whose primary concern is the people of their community, not themselves, their careers or their political party. Party politics have no place in our local councils."*

Once elected, they haven't operated in any way as a group.

Local Party

There are a number of groups that are in effect, a 'local party'. They have a manifesto and a leadership structure not unlike a political party. This comes with the advantages of using a model people understand but also the challenges of maintaining the structures that come with party rules and membership. These local parties tend to have formed around one, usually negative, campaign issue. The big challenge then is to move beyond that and survive and thrive once the issue is dealt with. It may also be more challenging to find positive aims if a group's origin is in negativity.

It's Our County in Hereford is a good example of a local party. They're open to members of all political parties and also those not members of any party, and as I write, they have a very impressive 9/53 county councillors and 12/17 city councillors. Similarly, Ashfield Independents won 30 out of 35 seats in their 2019 district election.

Partly local party
Some independent groups adopt aspects of the political party system and some adhere to a model more like Frome's: *"We have taken a slightly different route from IfF in that we have a traditional party structure that has a chair, treasurer, secretary, executive committee etc. We also maintain a membership and regular newsletter. Contact with voters will be vital when the next elections come round or we will face the criticism levelled at the traditional parties of being visible only when an election is due."*

Ideal Bradford

After the first election IfF adopted aspects of a manifesto in order to signal general intent. Others have done this from the start. Usually their aims are very broad e.g. 'We'll develop local partnerships to distribute resources fairly' and 'we'll back community projects with proven public support', which would be hard to object to. Often it picks up on a one-off issue where there's clearly massive public support, i.e. 'We'll continue to campaign against the proposed golf course.'

There are two main risks I see in overdeveloping a full manifesto. Firstly, you need the time and structures to make sure all the candidates really understand and agree on the issues. Secondly, there'll be people for and people against. A new group needs every vote going, and even something like 'we'll support projects enhancing a green and sustainable future', starts to put the group into a box.

To register as a minor political party or not?
Groups standing at parish/town level can choose whether to register as a minor political party; at higher levels, you have to register as a full political party. Either way, it costs £150 initially and £25 a year thereafter. The political party route requires significantly more information and ongoing administration.

Some groups have chosen not to register. The main advantage of registering is that the name of the group and its logo will be on the ballot paper and can't be used by anyone else. Without registering, the word 'independent' will usually appear after the candidate's name, so if there are other independents not in the group, you'll look to be in the same family.

However, at a local level up to six words can be added to the person's name. For example, 'retired banker', 'local gardener' or even something like 'Independent Arcadia working for you'. This last example helps identify the group, but there's nothing to stop any other independent using the same or a similar set of words. The only way to get a unique logo that no one else can pinch is by registering.

Are there risks to registering? As with so much of what we have learnt, there's a process as well as a product. Let's look at an example from Indy Monmouth: *"The group did not form a small minor political party but chose to be a loose affiliation of residents which, on reflection, the interviewees felt was a mistake as it didn't allow them to formalise their values and views and didn't give people 'something to sign up to'. In addition, it meant that everybody wanted the 'party' to be what they wanted it to be and it diluted the common message. It also meant that if they didn't get what they wanted they could cause trouble, which in turn prevented showing a united front."*

The lesson seems to be that even if there's a move towards a loose affiliation, thinking through what's required to become a registered group is a useful part of the process. Elsewhere, Liskeard, one of the earliest groups to take power in similar ways to Frome disbanded as a minor political party after the first electoral period. 'The council now has 15 independent councillors from a wide range of backgrounds, some of which were the rump of the initial group.'

Should independent groups accept candidates who are, or have been, councillors from the main political parties?

Another tricky area, with no right answer. Some groups are quite clear that membership of a political party precludes joining the independent group, others leave it up to the Ways of Working to deter the politicisation of the group. There are clearly cases of party councillors seeing the writing on the wall and 'offering their experience' to the new group primarily to keep their place on the council. The potential advantages of experience need to be weighed against a 'this is how we've always done it' attitude and possible defection back to their old party once elected. Most groups seem to take the line of 'a leopard can't change its spots'.

Party politicians often come with a promise of voters who will be loyal to them as individuals and thus increase the votes for independents. But will these loyal voters move their thinking to a new independent approach? You need to judge whether their previous allegiance will be more damaging than helpful to the new group as a whole, especially if their previous political identity is well known. In the first Frome election three of the seven not elected had been party councillors before, and their inclusion in the new group may have done more harm than good.

In a number of cases, groups who've not achieved a majority have sought alliances with supportive party councillors, and this seems a safer way to go.

In the 2019 elections there are a number of cases where ex-party councillors stood as independents, correctly reading the widespread rejection of party politics. There are now a number of coalitions between these councillors and those who campaigned as members of an independent group. It will be interesting to see how this works out and whether those seeking radical change are able to escape from the miasma of 'business as usual' that I fear could descend.

A note on standing at more than one level

IfF's stance on standing both in Frome and at other levels has been to gently discourage such thoughts and not to offer IfF's support to an individual wanting to also stand elsewhere. No one has yet done so. My experience is that 'multi-layer' councillors are rarely effective at the town level. They tend to give their time and energy to the higher levels and often fail to work democratically from the bottom up. Those from higher levels who attend key town meetings are a different matter, and to be welcomed.

There are a number of people who've successfully worked at both levels. Usually, these are individuals who've campaigned at the local level and then decided to step up as well. This was the case, for example, in Portishead in 2019 where the independents won all the town seats and four on the district and now sit as part of the ruling coalition, including one person in the cabinet.

Hopefully these individuals, being members of a group, will be able to provide much more useful links between the councils than they would sitting as lone independents.

When to come out

One of the points where there's little agreement among those we spoke with is this: when should you reveal that your group exists? Assuming a May election, the range has been from more than a year before to the very last moment before registrations must be in. The two key arguments are outlined below:

"Members have the philosophy that you need as long as possible to engage with your electorate. The longer timeframe has given them the opportunity to build trust with their electorate and in addition shake out any people who are not fully on board with the concept of independent politics. The longer you have the more people will get to know about you and the longer you have to build up your supporter base."

Portishead Independents

"The timescale from thinking about it to standing and to winning the election was incredibly short. The first meeting was on February 1st and we formally constituted as a Minor Political Party on March 1st."

The Haswells Community Party

During that time they put out a manifesto which set out how they would work, how they intended to give power back to the people of the area, leafleted the area and knocked on many doors. They think this narrow timescale worked to their advantage in that their approach was fresh and dynamic and people didn't have the chance to be bored by what they had to offer. The group went on to win 9/9 seats in the 2 May 2019 election.

It boils down to allowing time to really become well known and build a campaign vs not risking losing the energy and interest of candidates and potential voters. The ambush approach has the advantage of potentially wrong-footing the incumbent councillors and political parties, but a short campaign will need a higher profile to succeed.

A number of groups have been forming for a long time (up to a year), working out who they are and what they stand for, while not actually 'coming out' until quite late. There's clearly no right or wrong in this; I think it largely comes down to the energy and time candidates and their supporters have and the number of the electorate. Where the campaign is at a district, county or unitary authority level it clearly needs much longer as the number of candidates to be found, the electorate to inform and the areas to cover are much larger.

A word of warning.

It's well worth repeating that gathering candidates, with a show of hands, in a group meeting just before you have to register is extremely unlikely to produce a coherent group. It may produce a number of independent councillors, but will they be heading in the same direction?

"I don't think anyone is of the revolutionary bent I am, and the Indies with their Indy mayor are mostly getting absorbed by the system and performing as town councillors have always done.

"Know your candidates before you put them forward for election. Talk with them about politics, socialise with them, and really get to know them. If you elect someone who does not understand where you are coming from, your values and the concepts of independents working together will cause massive problems later. Three of ours have effectively left the party."

Indy Monmouth

CAMPAIGNING
Parish meetings and parish polls campaigning

The use of a parish meeting and parish poll were new to me before talking with two independent groups. In Desborough these little-known tools led to the incumbent council's resignation and (after elections) complete replacement by independents. Similarly a parish poll kick-started Portishead Independents' campaign to expose the existing council's shortcomings on their way to victory in 2019.

The Local Government Act states that there must be an Annual Parish Meeting for those on the electoral roll; this isn't the same as meetings of the parish council which is of those elected by those on the electoral roll. It should be organised and paid for by the council, and chaired by the council leader/mayor if they're present, but every resident has an equal right to speak, whether they're a councillor or not.

Less well known is that in addition any six residents who have the right to vote can call such a meeting at any time. This meeting can be used to discuss anything the people choose. What's more, the meeting can lead to a parish poll if ten people want a yes or no answer to a well-worded question (the returning officer at district level has to agree the wording). The outcome of the poll is no more and no less than an expression of the views of the electorate of the parish who've voted in the poll. It is not binding; however, if the meeting and poll express 'no confidence' in the council, as was the case in Portishead and Desborough, it will clearly demonstrate public disaffection, and this can influence councillors, the public and later campaigning.

"The parish meeting was very worthwhile. We had to turn people away as reached fire safety limit; nearly 7,000 individual views of the live-streamed video, including 1,200 watching on 'catch up' the next day. A local radio interview as well as press coverage, and we had strangers coming up to us thanking us for organising it. The current council chair commented beforehand "you have played a blinder – it's a win-win for you guys'. I'd recommend it as a great way to get publicity and show that you know what you are doing."

Portishead Independents

Being part of an independent movement

Each new group of independents faces similar kinds of questions:
- I don't know what you stand for.
- How can I trust you without a manifesto?
- It won't work without a political party structure.
- Political parties are a tried and tested way of doing things.

And so on. This last one is pretty staggering given the mess we're in, but most people seem to be resistant to change nonetheless.

So, is it helpful to use successful models, such as Frome, to show what can be done? And is there potential for independent groups to work together to get elected over a larger geographical area?

Two towns close to Frome have developed similar models. One gained a majority of independents in 2016 and all candidates were elected in the other, though not enough to take control. In both cases, there's been a sharing of ideas and support; however, both groups were keen to downplay the Frome connection. They wanted to show that their movement belonged to their own community; I'm sure this was wise. Two other independent groups where Frome was widely mentioned found this to be an easy target for criticism, perhaps because 'independent' implies 'independence'.
On the other hand, it is important to show that a model of an independent council with councillors working t together can really bring change is important. Perhaps as

more towns have a story to tell, this will become the norm; until then it's another slightly tricky balance. Making too much of using someone else's model is very different from giving some carefully-selected examples from a similar story.

There's a different issue around the working together as independent councils and groups once elected, which I come to below under 'municipalism'.

Coming together under one banner to get elected?

In 2019 a range of newly formed groups in Dorset worked under one banner, campaigning in a number of towns and two new unitary authorities. They shared branding as the Alliance for Local Living, ALL. ALL for Dorchester; ALL for Bournemouth/Poole/Christchurch etc. There are obvious advantages to this for campaigning, and it has great potential as long as the individual local groups are able to ensure they're identified with their own community.

THE MESSAGE
Social media

One of the very significant advantages that independent groups have because they're not tied to the messaging and rules of a political party is their better use of social media. Add to this their freedom to pull in people from the wider public, and they can often create a highly-skilled media team, willing and able to produce creative masterpieces (usually for free). This is well described by Portishead Independents, entering the fray in 2019 elections: *"Our main means of communication with the public and members is via Facebook. We've quickly added more than 800 followers. The last post reached 5,000 people with 2,500 clicking through for more information, with over 300 likes. We now have a bigger Facebook following than any of the national parties in the county."*

They note an interesting hierarchy of responses to Facebook posts. The best are posts about people, followed by voter education material, town issues, and finally details of pledges and positive news stories. Originally people responded to 'negative posts more than positive but that is now changing fast'.

In addition, they have a policy of not responding to attacks from other parties or the inevitable trolls, although they have had to ban a few people from posting on Facebook. Communications try to be as positive as possible, but this has sometimes proved impossible. Other groups would agree that by not responding to attacks or responding politely they make their detractors just look stupid. Just asking people to meet for a coffee normally makes detractors go quiet!

One group estimate that they spent about a third of their budget on Facebook advertising and consider it money well spent. They say it enabled them to engage with a large number of people at a relatively low cost and provide an insight into the demographic of supporters.

There's agreement that independent groups need to pull in more, new voters. Given that younger people tend not to vote, they're an obvious target, so social media is clearly important for this. But Facebook is now used more by older than younger people; younger generations have moved on to Instagram and other platforms. With all these mediums, short, punchy messages are what's required, and once produced they can be used in multiple ways.

Participation or representation?

I've commented on this conundrum in relation to Frome's experience. Not surprisingly it comes up with other groups too. Many of the groups who've taken power, or are trying to, have emerged from the community. They don't have connections to party ideology or ambitions of power outside their own towns. It therefore follows that they will look to include others in making decisions and tend towards participatory ways of doing things.

Universally, the successful groups that we talked to have all adopted greater engagement with the public as a basic policy. This usually starts with significantly changing the relationship between residents and the council.

However, ultimately councillors need to make decisions. Choosing when councillors should 'just do it' or seek to really engage with the public is one of the trickiest issues we face if we're to make local democracy work. Often decisions are quite simple and definitely don't need more consultation. The Lib Dems have a well-earned reputation for defaulting to endless consultation and not taking action.

My view is that people like to be asked, but if they are asked, the consultation must be followed with prompt action and keeping them informed. It's also far better to tell people why something didn't happen than to tell them nothing. Lack of follow up simply adds to the general cynicism around politics and councils.

AFTER ELECTION
Working with other councils

Frome is not alone in our struggle with other layers of governance. The bane of an ambitious town or parish council is the district's hold over planning decisions. Talking to others, most go for a pragmatic route from the start. 'Build relationships with other councils' was the message. Perhaps if we'd approached the issue like this, rather than waging war and eventually being forced to grovel, our district relationships might've been more fruitful.

Initial disappointment... what then?

What if you fail to take power or to have any significant number of councillors? In some cases, groups are going for the long game and expecting to win a few seats the first time round and then hang in for another election. Many of the groups I've followed are offering system change to voters and are pragmatic about how long this may take.

This was never my plan, and the energy of the most ambitious groups is for fundamental change. This can't be achieved without a majority of councillors (as independents or in a coalition), so what to do if the numbers don't stack after election day? It's an expensive and unpopular route to simply resign and go back to our day jobs.

In practice two things usually happen. Firstly, the few who get in do what they can within the system and remaining supporters continue to beaver away (or sometimes slowly drop off). The Cynon Valley Party is a good example of this: they had a hugely impressive campaign, with 10 candidates gaining 4,855 votes, and they came second in all but one seat. However, they only actually won a single seat. Their supporters must then wait for the next election to try again.

Secondly, the group shifts energy to community activity, which it runs in parallel with council work. Often this is ignored and certainly not supported by the council, but the group does it anyway. For example, in Monmouth the minority independent group organised a hugely successful Lantern Parade bringing over 2,000 people into the town – 10 times more than a similar event the previous year. 'We received a lot of grief from the council and others when trying to set it up, being told it was going to fail etc. and quibbling over minor details.'

Where groups have emerged from the community, they effectively return to this work, though now it's associated with the group in preparation for the next election. For example, the Wells Independents (WIN) set up Wells SOUP after their disappointing results in 2015. SOUP provides an excellent soup for £5 and invited community groups then bid for the profit. Around 100 people attend each event, and £8,000 has been distributed to 50 local groups. This is clearly branded back to Wells

Independents, and undoubtedly contributed to WIN's results in 2019 when all five of their candidates were elected.

Is it worth all the effort?

"In 2004, a group of us organised a slate of independent candidates in Cardiff in protest at the uselessness of all the main parties on the city council. Although we played a useful role in publicising the situation which led to a change in the administration, and had an enjoyable experience in the process, none of us were elected and we learnt the limitations of independent politics in our current system."

Looking at the 2019 results it's certainly possible for large numbers of towns and parishes to be run by groups of independent councillors working together for their communities. 40 per cent of those I followed are now in complete control. Whether significant numbers will be ambitious and effective, we won't know for a few years, but the models of Buckfastleigh, Bradford on Avon, Alderley Edge, Frome and others bode well.

Hopefully the National Association of Local Councils and the Ministry of Communities and Local Government will recognise this groundswell of engagement for what it is: not a form of opposition to be derided or feared but people working together to improve the wellbeing and environment in their communities (and who need all the support they can get).

8. Attention from continental Europe and further afield

Annabelle and Peter Macfadyen in Aarhus, Denmark

In 2014 sales of *Flatpack Democracy* and various additional articles and talks I've given have helped stimulate interest in Frome's politics. Frome also won a number of awards and clearly become a place to go to rather than avoid. However, in 2015 when IfF won all 17 seats and *The Guardian* printed a two-page article, it brought a significantly greater attention to Frome's politics.

I now realise that the main reason for this was that we'd become material for case studies rather than an engine for change. I've described elsewhere how IfF has changed the way politics is done in Frome with a mass of attributable achievements. So, unsurprisingly, there have been a number of films, documentaries and articles about us.

The surprise has been that many have been from other countries, for example Denmark, Belgium, France, Spain, and, even more surprisingly, South Korea. Indeed, our exploits are probably better known about in Denmark than in much of Frome. Partly, there's a degree of 'political tourism' going on, but there's also probably a desire to better understand what lessons can be learnt. As I write, parties of 40 Belgians and around 20 Danes are booked in to visit Frome, building on what we've achieved but also adding to the local economy.

My feelings oscillate regarding Frome's international fame. Sometimes the coverage of Frome's story seems like a lot of froth; other times I can see how what we've achieved is really inspiring for others. There's such extreme frustration throughout Europe with the lack of democracy, so if we can stimulate ideas and conversations that lead to change then that must be a good thing.

Denmark

At the heart of IfF lies its core values and ethos, and how these are encapsulated in the Ways of Working. It was these that attracted connections with the Alternativet party in Denmark. Alternativet is a values-led party that had, at one point, 10 MPs at national level. Our joint interest was in whether or not having a manifesto actually leads to more participative democracy. This has led to a series of positive exchanges, meetings and conversations with Alternativet over the last four years. At this point, I feel it's worth mentioning Alternativet's six core values:
- Courage
- Generosity
- Transparency
- Humility
- Humour
- Empathy

These questions about democratic structure and values have also led to a great deal of academic research, both here and in Denmark.

There's one such study, by Emil Husted, Professor of Business and Politics in the Copenhagen Business School. Emil has researched and written widely on the relationship between organisational values and commitment to a political party. His contention is that carefully-created values tend to fall into two groups: those that promote creativity and openness to change and those that promote courtesy and cooperation. If this mix is present, Emil concludes, then it's possible to maintain the commitment and engagement of members who would otherwise be marginalised by the dominant ideas that inevitably emerge as the group or party ages.

I think this holds true for IfF. Certainly, with our large group of councillors it's been essential to enable those with specific ideas that could be deemed peripheral to our main aims to pursue these while also maintaining some 'big ideas' at the core.

Belgium, Holland and the Flatpack Party

Given that people in Belgium have bought a significant number of copies of *Flatpack Democracy* (though the Dutch translation sadly hit the rocks), it seems fair to share some comments from their experiences. I've had many conversations with other groups in different European countries, and the deplorable state of local-level democracy is pretty much universal. Below are the thoughts of some of those attempting to affect change in Belgium at a local level: *"Only half of the Dutch people show up at elections, and alarmingly few residents want to become councillors themselves. The local solidarity that village politics brought us has disappeared. The local politician is becoming less and less accessible to citizens. How is that possible, and how do we get municipal politics back on track?*

"It's quite an amazing (and large) group of people that have all picked up on the same idea that you started years ago. Expanding it to city scale is challenging, but I dare say that we're pretty much ready (one of our upcoming training courses is 'diplomatic negotiations', to give you an idea). Most incredibly though, there has not been a single instance of in-group conflict. It's hard to explain, but it just seemed the value system 'clicked'."

Citizens of Grobbendonk and Bouwel

In Antwerp a 'Flatpack Party' has emerged. They've produced the most radical evolution to Ways of Working in the form of a Democratic Oath. It owes its existence partly to the Belgan legal rules related to setting up parties in which the oath becomes a legal document. Some of its sections I quote below are magnificently ambitious and would certainly change the face of politics if enacted:

- I will respect and improve all existing democratic achievements and will share my knowledge and experience with those who will follow after me.
- At all times, I will submit policies and decisions to a group of citizens of the broadest possible diversity and I will respect, defend and apply the outcome of this consultation within the limits of my legal abilities.
- I will not feign knowledge, spread false information or in any way obstruct the process of correctly and thoroughly informing the citizens that I represent. If necessary, I will call on experts or conduct research, in which case all the resulting information will be rendered fully accessible to the public.

- Under no circumstances will I issue laws that influence the process of political decision-making, political tenures or remuneration, without the explicit approval of the citizens by vote.
- My political actions will be aimed at the future of mankind and therefore a better environment for future generations will always take precedence over short term benefits for the current generation.

The Antwerp group, along with others in Belgium, gained an extraordinary number of votes in late 2018, but no seats. This was mainly put down to an effective collaboration between the existing parties, who worked together to create rules and obstacles to exclude them. They managed this even though they were, on paper at least, in opposition to each other. In their own words (in reply to an email I sent them after their elections to ask them how they'd got on): *"Sorry that I didn't inform you sooner, we had a great party last night... No, we did not win any seats. Just 0.7% short. The Belgian system is not favourable for starting movements. The first seat is a very costly one. After that it goes much faster: for the first seat we need 600 votes, the next only 300 votes more and with 1,900 votes you have six seats. An absolute majority needs about 3,000 votes.*

We are not disappointed! Just a pity we don't have a seat. Anyway, we will continue to spread the word and the system with passion and try to get more people on board. It's difficult to change people's mindset after 40 something years of party indoctrination."

The Belgians are looking to put together a 'hodge-podge coalition of organisations working on transparency, direct democracy or e-democracy, referenda, sortition and of course a bunch of 'Flatpackers'.

Attention from the other side of the world

We've even sent copies of Flatpack Democracy to New Zealand. This email is a typical response: *"We are in New Zealand and have our local body elections on 12 October 2019. We used Flatpack Democracy for the 2016 elections and the resistance to amalgamation of the 3 councils in our area (rural north of Wellington City called the Wairarapa) in 2017 and won with 59% (75% in our district of Carterton).*

For your interest, I have attached a Discussion Paper for what we want to achieve in the 2019 elections calling this campaign 'Revitalise community-led democracy'.

Thankfully party-based candidates have never been part of rural New Zealand councils (they are more so in cities), but we have an issue with the council executives taking over control by undermining and weakening governance for their own agendas – thus we are having to protect democracy. As you say, 'There has never been a more important time to reclaim politics than now'."

9. Mayor power ego

From the Mayoral Chains
(Frome Area Leg Club)
photographic series by
David Partner

One of the key elements of the IfF approach is we recognise that we all, councillors and staff, need to look widely for inspiration and information. In writing this book I wanted to touch on some key issues, including both power and gender; however, I'm anything but an expert in either of these areas. My idea is that even if you're not equipped to solve the problem, exposing it may remove some of its damaging impact and will allow others the option of action. I'll set out here some of my personal experiences and invite later exploration and discussion through the *Flatpack Democracy* website.

A collection of issues around power can be especially well illustrated by my time as Mayor of Frome. I wrote *Flatpack Democracy* half way through the first four-year period, when IfF had a majority in the council. It was in 2014, the last year of that term that I was elected mayor.

My own mayoral story

At its simplest level, the mayor is the chairperson of the council, elected by the councillors. Some councils choose to elevate the title to 'mayor' and add a number of performance roles in which this person represents the town. A big part of that role is to communicate the views and decisions of the council rather than the mayor's personal thoughts. Inevitably, the higher profile means the mayor is the person the public often turn to in order to comment, praise or complain.

By the time I became Mayor of Frome there were well-populated mayoral Facebook and Twitter accounts. Subsequent mayors have added a newsletter. As with all IfF communication, I kept the content of these social media channels light, positive and upbeat.

I was initially reluctant to step forward as mayor but was persuaded by the views of my predecessors that it would be a fantastic way to meet people outside my normal circles and deepen my understanding of the Frome community at large. I was also aware that being mayor would be a good opportunity to broadly promote my own areas of interest, in the environment and in breaking down barriers between the public and the council. These opportunities came together in what became a central focus of my year: The Mayor's Chains.

The mayor's chains

After one of my very first council meetings there was a formal complaint in relation to my wearing shorts for a meeting. That they were very smart shorts with a matching well-ironed shirt seemed to cut no ice. I've always abhorred the use of custom and tradition by people in power to exclude those who don't know the rules. The way most councils operate is a prime example of this, with rules and regulations that include some and exclude most. There's a place for tradition and ceremony, but it's not in the everyday working of a council trying to do its best to enable and empower the public. However, there are those who think otherwise: *"…a dress code should be put in place… we are elected members and should dress appropriately … we need to respect the Mayoral Chain…"*

Cllr Mike Ryan, Newton Abbot, 2018

In my first week I was invited to St John's School to talk to their Green Panthers Group, and I took the chain along. Our conversation included the probable working conditions of the miners who extracted the gold for the chain. The children offered to make me an ethical alternative, which I obviously accepted. A week later I opened the school fete in my new chain made of a bike tyre, bottle tops and other recycled jewels.

The Lego Club then asked if they could make me a chain, and one thing led to another. The chains became a record of Frome's active communities, a snapshot of the vibrancy and creativity that emerges when people are given licence to play. The idea was to emphasise that the council and the mayor are just a part of the community and the status and power associated with the traditional chain can and should be questioned.

The chains fell into groups that covered most of the council's work. The environment was represented with the world's first solar-powered chain and a chain made by a Frome Plastic Recycling Company; food was represented by three chains that went on to either be eaten or composted; health and wellbeing was showcased with the Leg Club's creation around ulcer treatment; there were a range of creative offerings to represent the Arts; Amnesty's barbed wire and candle chain – that was the hardest to wear and finally one representing the community toilet scheme. The original gold chain still made many appearances; I wore it when appropriate – even I'm not fool enough to be too creative with the Remembrance Day Service.

A Frome photographer, David Partner, asked to record the chains as they emerged. His previous work includes '*Heads of Government*', which was exhibited in the National Portrait Gallery. Mount Gallery, a new Frome business, asked to frame these pictures, and by the end of my year 24 full-size chain portraits formed an exhibition. This was shown in Frome and later in the old Davenport mayoral chambers. The exhibition is still available today.

All this chainery aimed to raise the status of the clubs, groups and small businesses of Frome. I will admit to a moment of mixed feelings when I entered a room full of large portraits of myself. I always saw myself as the background for the chains. I had a similar moment to think about ego when I stepped onstage to introduce a group of speakers and everyone clapped. I'd done nothing and yet the people loved me! Our relationship with power and the dangers of becoming addicted to it run through councils even at this lower level.

I think it's incredibly important to prick the bubble of ego and power, but even easier to overlook the dangers. In two cases I know well where majority independent councils have been elected, their work has been catastrophically affected by the new mayor belatedly discovering an ego. All too easily this merges into the abuse of power, the results of which may not be as serious as in higher levels of government but are still significant. Being aware of these pitfalls is important if we are to build some form of democracy in which most people can feel included and engaged.

I should mention Sheffield's recent Lord Mayor before leaving this section. Magid Magid, who entered the UK as a Somali refugee, has taken his role seriously while also looking to make it more accessible. There were complaints about his choice of music for his inauguration ceremony – 'The Imperial March' from *Star Wars* – but we can't complain about lack of political engagement while failing to embrace change. His approach has worked well enough to lead onto his election as Yorkshire's first Green MEP.

Conflict and power

My fellow IfF councillor Jean Boulton wrote the following:

"This tolerance of diversity and style has in the main resulted in harmony and good working relationships, which is not to say that everything always goes smoothly. There are times when some people feel excluded or unable to find a way in; there are times when conflict breaks out; there are times when 'power' is held through who is 'in the know', who sets the agenda, who (and where) decisions are in effect made or 'rehearsed'. And, paradoxically, in a desire not to end up with conflict we may have developed a culture where it can be hard to disagree and surface frustrations.

"Of course this is compounded where there is an active desire not to share power. I suspect this was most noticeable when new IfF councillors wanted to enter into policy areas which were already up and running. At times there was a reluctance to spend time revisiting early decisions, although this would have enabled a way in for the new councillors.

"Without a formal opposition, the second IfF period has had a slightly strange dynamic at times. We have had healthy debate and disagreement but perhaps because we were elected under one banner, there have been times where real disagreement has been avoided for the sake of harmony. Discussion around Ways of Working would do well to include how conflict will be handled when it comes up, in part to encourage that to happen. For me this would not be a formal 'conflict procedure' but would include guidance as to where and when these issues could be dealt with in a facilitated space."

Hidden power

There are obvious points where power is held by virtue of the role in a council's structure. In Frome we chose to have an annually elected leader of the council as well as a mayor. This was because we felt there'd be more chance of real discussion with the leaders at district and county level if they had a traditional structure to cling on to. We also hoped it would separate the public duties of the mayor from those of the leader in managing the town council. In addition we have the deputy mayor and the chairs and deputies of the two committees.

In parallel, there's the town clerk. This individual is often very powerful: not only can they decide what is and what isn't easily seen, but they're responsible for producing meeting agendas. While the standing orders (the rules) are set out by a mix of central government and the council, the clerk usually 'helps' interpret them. This is usually genuinely helpful, but there's obviously potential for guiding the rules in a particular direction.

In most councils no one seems to really manage the town clerk; this is part of the reason that, in my view, they often have way too much power. Where there is some management of the clerk, it often falls to the mayor. We instigated annual appraisals and ongoing management of the clerk by the leader in close association with others. Over the years as a councillor I became more aware of issues of power. For a group to function really well and achieve its ambitions, I think it can help enormously to have open discussions on the different roles each of us play and how people make decisions. This would inevitably include discussions about power, who holds it and how it's exercised. Problems arise when people find they've been disempowered, either deliberately or not, and don't understand how or why.

With 17 councillors in the second IfF administration, it was never going to be possible or sensible to have all of the councillors involved equally. Some people successfully took on specialist roles but we effectively lost others because we failed to understand how power and personality impacted on them.

My key point is that if a group of councillors is to achieve more than turning up every few months and doing what the clerk tells them, they need to look carefully and transparently at power and decision making.

Finally, I want to refer to the Civil Society Futures 2018 independent inquiry, which focused on 'shifting power, bridging divides and transforming society'. In engaging with other councils, I've often come up against 'old power' – held by a few and, once gained, jealously guarded. The inquiry talks of 'new power' that's 'open, participatory and peer driven'. It also states, 'the goal with new power is not to hoard it but to channel it'. Power shouldn't be about 'power over' but 'power with' the community.

Gender in politics

Discussion of power leads into comments about gender, because it's clear we have so far failed, not just as IfF but as a society, to enable women to fully participate. My comments here come from a life's work in social justice but focus on the last few years as an IfF councillor, especially the last four years.

With regard to our interaction with the public, I feel we could have done much more to ensure greater opportunity for those less able to participate. As chair and facilitator of so many meetings in the last few years, I've seen how women often find the traditional systems and structures harder to engage with than men (an observation backed up by innumerable studies).

Closer to home, the second IfF group of councillors had 8/17 women, so not a bad gender split. But it's much more than a question of mere numbers. To varying degrees, many of the women councillors reported they'd not found it easy to be heard or included in discussions, which led to them being less effective in their roles. Our discussions and actions steered away from touching on the social and cultural aspects of gender in relation to political power and influence such that we never tackled the situation. This was, I felt, to the detriment of the council as a whole and at a cost to our potential and effectiveness.

I'd put this lack of engagement on the issue of gender down to lack of knowledge, commitment and time rather than malevolent intent. To properly engage with gender is a huge leap for a group of individuals, voluntary councillors with limited personal and council time or resources. There was regular discussion of 'whether women are present', but such simplification meant that we missed opportunities for more radical change or new approaches. We could have made different decisions in relation to what was on the agenda, for example looking more deeply at power, as I suggest above, especially at the regular 'party conferences' where big issues were tackled.

Over the full eight years of IfF, men held more of the key roles than women. The campaigns have been run by men. The convenors were always men. The leadership role was held by men in seven out of eight years. The external facilitators we brought in were always men. Latterly, although five out of six of the councils middle-layer managers were women they were managed by the two men at the top. Too often there were key meetings of senior staff and councillors that were all male. To change this would have required a real intent, which for whatever reason we've never had. Personally, I would have liked to see a move towards the strategic 'feminising of politics', something that's more powerful than simply getting more women into positions of political power. Feminisation of politics is much more nuanced. A good illustration of this is the new wave of energy channelled into municipalism in Spain as a direct reaction to austerity.

In Barcelona and Madrid, where the new mayors are women, there's been a goal to deepen democracy and empower more people through promoting 'feminine' ways of doing. This has meant working towards increased and enhanced collaboration, dialogue and non-hierarchical practice, resulting in a politics based on values and practices – a politics that puts an emphasis on everyday life, relationships, the role of the community and the common good.

The core values that make up IfF 's Ways of Working dovetail well with the direction of this municipalisation and its empowerment of women, both in the roles they hold and in the underlying principles of activities.

Engaging women

As so often in this story, a reaction to an issue, in this case patriarchy, came from the community. It was noticed that in a mixed gender group of IfF councillors engaged in a discussion, the women were steadily less and less engaged. As a result of this, in 2014, a working group emerged with the title '*Engaging Women*'. The group aimed to '...encourage and support the voice of women in our local community to bring together a group of positive women who don't just want to talk about it but want to make it happen'.

After a series of informal meetings the focus narrowed on supporting and encouraging women to stand in the 2015 town council elections. This was a very successful project, with a number of women who'd either not previously considered standing or who needed more support to consider doing so subsequently being elected.

The group continued to promote events over the next four years, and in late 2018 they held another meeting to encourage women to stand in the town council elections. This time they looked both for potential candidates and for those who could offer on-going support in the areas women might find challenging or lack skills or confidence, for example public speaking, as well as helping with practical issues like childcare. The offer was especially aimed at women with no experience in local politics to help 'give a voice to all women of Frome by ensuring we have a say in the way we do politics in our town'. While the founders of *Engaging Women* have links to IfF, their offer was open to anyone wishing to stand for any political party.

Incidentally, as new councils have emerged with larger numbers of younger people and women, providing a wider range of expenses to allow attendance at meetings and events is becoming an important factor.

Initiatives like *Engaging Women* are to be warmly welcomed. The group undoubtedly helped towards equal numbers of men and women in the 2015 town election and in supporting others to stand in 2019. Some women who decided not to stand in 2019 have expressed a desire to be involved in 2023.

My conclusion in relation to the issues of power (and associated ego), gender and other discriminations, is that having them out there, exposed and discussed is essential as a first step to redressing the balance.

Some things are usually simple, like ensuring there's never a male-only panel and that key decisions are made by groups with a gender mix. However, as noted above, it's not as easy as ensuring equal numbers. The current Labour Party is rightly proud of an equal gender mix in the Shadow Cabinet, but the top three jobs are held by men. Democracy has a habit of producing annoying gender imbalances if posts are chosen individually – the 2019 IfF council's first meeting elected men to the three top roles.

It's so easy to make assumptions, especially about people we think we know but also of ourselves. Greater awareness of my own bias would certainly have helped avoid some damaging comments I made and things I did. While staff should have 'gender equality training' and training in allied areas, this will only be the start of bringing about the necessary cultural change.

The old fashioned status of councillors allows free rein for behaviour that can do so much damage. The easiest starting point is to change the rules and ensure greater informality and accessibility. Anything to reduce the distance between people and power has to be welcomed – hence the new takes on the mayor's chains.

10. So what? A reality check

The author at a presentation by All for Dorset

Introduction

Inevitably *Flatpack Democracy 2.0* has a strong element of autobiography. Although being a councillor is not the only thing I've done since 2011, it has been a central part of my life. It's taken me into all kinds of new spaces and places. This chapter aims to put the work of IfF and Frome Town Council over the last eight years into that wider context. I've always been looking for how ideas that spring from IfF might both change people's day-to-day lives in Frome and also impact on a wider democratic agenda.

I came to being a councillor after having established Sustainable Frome, which has at its core recognition that climate breakdown will change everything. From that came an understanding that our current political systems are totally incapable of either stopping the causes of climate breakdown or preparing people to face what lies ahead. Watching parliament trying to deal with Brexit has proved to me the total inability of our politicians to move beyond political expediency or personal gain and for current political systems to deal sensibly with these highly complex situations.

So, does this mean we've been fiddling in Frome while the planet burns? If so, can that fiddling be put to good use here and elsewhere? What role can a town council possibly play? And what might be the options for massively upping the game? I'll summarise my view of whether IfF has met its main aims. Then whether it is possible for groups of individuals to breathe new life into their communities through a vibrant council and how far that can be pushed.

The starting point

Any council wishing to up its game must remember it sits within a national and regional political context. I'm not going to rehash here the full rant I've written in other places and spoken about at innumerable meetings, except for a few key points:
- We've arrived at a political system that is totally unfit for most purposes.
- Our UK system may be marginally better than some countries, but it's definitely worse than many.
- Overall, 'democracy' is a fiction for the vast majority of humankind.

In Britain, only a tiny number of people in a few marginal seats decide who runs the country. Whoever's in power, the majority of people are not represented. Seeking and retaining power becomes the most important factor for individuals and parties. On top of all that our confrontational system fails us completely when there are complex systemic challenges to deal with.

So while a new poll by the Conservative-leaning Daily Express finds 72% of people are ready for a complete overhaul of British politics, the system has no way – or no will – to do so. Astonishingly, since the Brexit referendum, the UK has spawned no fewer than 90 new political parties. But with the notably unpleasant exception of the Brexit Party, the system prevents any of them from wielding any significant influence despite their splendid names, like 'Engage', 'Aspire' and the 'Ninety-Nine Percent Party'. At a national level we're stuck.

Local government

Perhaps while this debacle continues, true representation can happen outside central government? Perhaps us worker bees can keep the hive running even if the queen is failing in her duties? After all, local authorities still deliver roughly a quarter of all public services.

Sadly, financial stringency means they do so overwhelmingly as an agency of central government. British local government is now so marginalised it's off the international graph for centralisation. It controls a derisory 1.6% of GDP compared to 6% in France, 11% in Germany and 16% in Sweden. Its financing equates to that of a failed state.

Given this lack of resources, it's no surprise that there's a real struggle to excite anyone's engagement in local government. The counties, districts and unitary authorities are desperately struggling to provide the services required of them and often failing, with increasingly inadequate funding. Are we then surprised that over a quarter of those eligible don't even register to vote? When there isn't a national election on the same day, only around one third of registered voters actually vote in towns and parishes, and the majority of wards are not even contested. Where there are councillors, two thirds are men, mostly elderly, who stay in post on average over ten years. Young people and black and ethnic minorities are less and less likely to engage.

HAS THE FROME EXPERIENCE REDUCED THE PAIN?

Eight years ago I stepped into the scenario described above. Partially enthused by the opportunity of localism, I was also beginning to be aware of the pain austerity was about to inflict. In Chapter 2 I set out the three main factors behind IfF's emergence. Did our response to each of these make any difference at either the local or the district, county and national level?

Getting rid of party politics at a local level

After two elections there were no Frome councillors elected based on membership of a national political party. In 2019 Frome elected another full set of independents. I strongly believe that this has allowed us to serve Frome better for three reasons:

1. By drawing candidates from a much wider pool we simply have better people to choose from. The parties can only draw from their membership, and less than 2% of registered voters are members of a political party, even with an increase (and subsequent decline) in Labour members. Additionally, in the Labour and Conservative Parties only a third of members are women.

2. Somewhere in their baggage, those who come with a party mandate put the ideology of that party first. On the other hand, people who've come forward for IfF have a primary focus on what they can do for Frome. They represent a wide range of views and come with many skills and experiences. They're not (yet) a perfectly representative group, but they're much better than those taken from any party membership.

3. Rather than simply wrap yourself in a familiar colour to gain a vote, an independent has to put forward what they'll bring to the role. That's more challenging and more honest. Over 27,000 votes were cast in the 2015 election: they were all for people who said 'this is who I am and this is how I will behave'.

Getting rid of party politics was IfF's first challenge, and initially I thought it was the main one. I still think it was incredibly important for Frome and often is elsewhere, but experience now shows that it was just the first hurdle to change the way local government operates.

However, I think Frome is ahead of the game in recognising that at a local level the party political system is redundant; elsewhere, of course, I've bemoaned our inadequate system of democracy at a national level. At the heart of this is the failure of political parties. They were formed in an earlier world of command and control. As Neil Lawson, of Compass puts it: *"The shift from the vertical to the horizontal disperses power and information. It creates a cultural context in which people are more likely to have multiple identities rather than a single focus. The whole conception of the Party needs to be turned on its head. The job of the political leader is not to acquire power, or the trappings of it, to determine which levers to pull for the people, but to use democratic power to provide the platforms and spaces for collective self-actualisation. This doesn't negate the need for lever pulling or the management and administration of routine affairs of state, it is to say that the abiding purpose of gaining office is to help make citizens more powerful."*

And I would argue this is exactly what we have been trying to do in Frome.

Tackling austerity because no one else is going to

It's stretching the point to say that the collapse of the middle levels of local government and the lack of funds provides local communities with real opportunity. The basic premise of paying taxes and receiving services, which leads to decreasing real engagement, is flawed. We've now been forced into doing more things for ourselves, and some of them are done better simply because the local community understands its own needs better. Equally, there's a wellbeing element to this: the lives of those getting stuck in, creating new relationships and taking more responsibility for their own services are arguably enriched by the process.

If that starts to sound like an apology for austerity, don't be fooled: I strongly believe that most people are significantly worse off as a result of government cuts to services. Reduced family, youth and mental health support come to mind; these are all areas where town councils are struggling to support significant change, having been forced to take action when services disappeared.

Frome, tucked away as it is and neglected by the district and county, has always had a bolshy stance. A town council that's saying, 'who's going to stop you?' and 'better to seek forgiveness than ask permission' has helped create an environment in which risks are taken and ideas and action can flourish.

We've certainly not beaten austerity. But there's a strong case to be made that the IfF-led town councils have played a part in reducing the impact through creating more of a 'can do' culture.

Did we use localism to 'give power to the man and woman on the street'?

David Cameron promised to 'take power from the political elite and give it to the man and woman on the street'. Frankly, it wasn't his worst idea!

The Localism Act let us claim the 'Powers of General Competence' so we could do anything that wasn't illegal. This in turn freed our sense of enterprise and enabled the borrowing that's fed into some of IfF's most visible and effective projects. However, I suspect we'd have found a way to do much of this stuff anyway. It also enabled the Neighbourhood Plan, which the district has to 'take into account' when making its decisions. The Plan has been useful as a process of engagement, but I question its deeper impact.

Most painfully, the expectation that significant money associated with new housing developments would come to the town and council proved unfounded. The money has been spent instead by the district council to keep them afloat in the face of drastic government cuts. It didn't have to be like this. Elsewhere, localism has clearly helped move assets from county and district to town and parish level. Cornwall County Council, for example, has used the Localism Act to help devolve the management of 75 public assets (pools, green spaces, play areas, historic buildings, libraries and car parks) to towns, importantly with resources to support them.

My Pickles moment

In 2015 I had an improbable conversation with the then Secretary of State for Local Government, Eric Pickles, about the quandary relating to ambitious councils such as Frome's. As a fervent promoter of localism, he applauded our achievements, but he was unable to escape the conundrum of how to move localism 'down' to Frome, without also having to do so to other town and parish councils far less capable and ambitious than ours.

If the British Government isn't prepared to put resources into strengthening local communities then localism will always be just a nice vote-winning idea rather than something that might actually happen. Building such capacity needs long term commitment and funding, which means raising taxes – never a vote winner. The council has taken advantage of most of the main offerings of the Localism Act to little overall benefit. My conclusion is that localism was a smokescreen to hide the ideology of the austerity-led destruction of local services. It inadvertently helped our creativity and ambition but has done little else .

HOW CAN WE BUILD ON WHAT HAS BEEN ACHIEVED?

So far, I've awarded the IfF experiment high marks for changing the system at a local level, making some real differences and supporting others to fight off the worst impacts of austerity. I've implied that this is nowhere near enough to bring long-lasting change. And I've mentioned climate breakdown to remind us of the huge challenges ahead.

Over the last few years I've come across a whole range of activities that could be used to up the game for councils and communities like Frome's. I've put them into four categories together with some ideas taken from Frome's experiences over the last eight years. As ever, you can pick n' mix from any of the following:

- **Option 1** – tweak the existing systems a bit
- **Option 2** – implement significant new ways to strengthen the local government/community relationship
- **Option 3** – open up engagement
- **Option 4** – change the system.

1) Tweak the existing systems a bit
Embedding the ethos.
If the new Frome Town Council continues to do the following, then perhaps we'll learn more about how to do these things well, creating a more resilient and better functioning community:

- Work to prevent problems rather than simply to manage them.
- Listen to the community
- Connect and signpost instead of just doing things for people
- Move from service-driven to people-driven action
- Re-configure people as the solution rather than the problem
- Build relationships as an essential precursor to any intervention.

If this way of thinking and acting is spread to other councils through successful events like Breaking the Mould (detailed in Chapter 5) then we could move towards a functioning level of local government in a relatively short timescale. However, they would need to be funded and resourced by the National Association of Local Government (NALC) and the Department for Communities, who to date have proven unhelpful.

All this could be easily arranged. Since 2019, more than 20 town councils are already on a similar path of ambitious independence. Rolled out nationally it would make a real difference to a huge number of people's lives at a community level. It just means allocating minimal resources and creating a real desire for change.

Working to support politicians at district, county and national level

In my naivety, I thought it might be possible to support elected politicians higher up the system, despite their party allegiances. Surely it makes sense to see them as colleagues to work with in order to achieve the best for the people we all represent? I have said enough about how impossible we found this at the district and county level. I've also had regular meetings with our MP in the hope that personal conversations might be a way in. He seems to me largely lost in a morass of emails and minutiae. I am sure he does a great job of sorting people's housing benefit claims, but in a centralised cabinet system he ultimately has little more power than I do.

As a council and as individuals we lobby national government for change, replying to endless responses and petitions. I have no evidence that any of this has made the slightest difference. Worse than being a waste of time, it makes us think we've taken positive action when all we've done is help maintain the status quo.

So will change ever come from 'higher levels'? 'Localism', or versions of it, turn up on every party manifesto; It's seen as a vote winner. Predictably, it then disappears when they take power.

The question is this: can local councils do more without a real form of localism in place? Leicester University's ' *Voice of the Councillor*' report concludes that: *'It is wholly wrong to see parish councillors as somehow a lesser form of councillor to their counterparts on other levels of government. Parish councillors require the same support mechanisms, training, research and administrative infrastructure as principal authority councillors.'*

Their recommendations conclude that parish councillors should have the right to demand and receive information and data, in a usable form, from the council of which they are a member and from a range of external bodi es. And those councils should structure themselves organisationally so as to support all councillors in the work they do. It would not be a huge tweak to see this happen. Town Clerks have a whole structure of training and support. Building councillor capacity would quickly allow further changes of the kind Eric Pickles envisaged but could not see how to enable.

2) Implement new ways to strengthen the local government/ community relationship

With the impacts of austerity now so catastrophic, there are some great examples of emerging councils taking action. While these examples have been initiated at higher levels than Frome, the core of their ideas might be adapted to town and parish level. Each of these is well documented elsewhere and well worth checking out.

The Wigan Deal

This is an informal agreement between the council and everyone who lives or works in Wigan to work together to create a better borough. Their slogan is 'Believe in Wigan'. The council has committed to a series of pledges and in return asks residents and businesses to play their part too. Within the first year the council saved £115m, supporting people to maintain services.

The Preston Model

The 'Preston Model' is a term applied to how the council, its anchor institutions and other partners are implementing the principles of Community Wealth Building. At its core is the principle of spending money as close to home as possible. This has meant that amid historically drastic cuts and declining budgets the amount spent locally has gone up. The six main local public bodies spent £38m in Preston in 2013; by 2017 the figure was £111m. Where other authorities privatise, Preston grows its own businesses. It's even created worker-owned co-operatives.

Barnsley Council

The experience of Barnsley Council in devolving power to local wards is especially interesting. They've invested in training councillors and given a strong steer to drop party politics at ward level. The process has proved popular, demonstrating that even political parties can take this route.

Needing to find 50% cuts over five years but not wanting to slash and burn services, they've chosen to work with citizens rather than simply do things for them. The council lists all the approaches familiar in Frome. For example, it's provided £100,000 per ward to fund local projects and services, with residents, community groups and councillors sitting on funded 'Ward Alliances'. It has also established 'Neighbourhood Networks' run by host voluntary organisations.

Barnsley calculates an average £25 in social return per £1 invested; around 94% of money spent has been kept in the local economy, together with a range of other benefits.

The Kirklees Democracy Model

This model has come at the challenges differently with a firm focus on democracy. They commissioned research on how to change the relationship between the people and local government, ensuring it was carried out with the maximum participation. Their 2017 report then established a whole range of ways both local and national democracy could develop over the next decade. Crucially, the council moved quickly to enact many of the recommendations.

Dagenham

Dagenham is faced with an evil mix of poverty, far-right politics and collapse at many levels. They commissioned a £7m five-year experiment called 'Every One, Every Day'. Based on existing successful community projects, the key features to support new projects were that they:

- Demand little time or commitment from local people
- Have little or no financial cost
- Are close to people's homes
- Are open to everyone
- Are designed to attract talent rather than to meet particular needs
- Create physical and visible infrastructure.

In other words, they foster simple projects that immediately improve people's lives. The projects all have a strong social focus. However, this isn't about entrepreneurial capitalism but about small scale projects that can have an immediate impact, like football coaching in the streets and tuition for spoken-word poets.

There must be many more examples like these. If district and county-level councils choose to do so, they can quite quickly change the lives of significant numbers of people. But spot that word 'change'; too many people in local government seem paralysed by the idea of tearing up the model and taking risks.

3) Open up engagement

The vast majority of councils at the town and parish levels, and their equivalent in other countries, fail to represent and to facilitate true participation. Historically it might possibly have made sense for a few men in a smoke-filled room to decide for the rest of us: basically the system said, 'elect me and I will make all decisions for you'. The modern version of this trope, 'vote for me and if elected I will do what I am told by the party leadership, possibly following a manifesto created by a few people a long time ago and far away' is clearly not fit for purpose now.

In direct contrast, Frome Town Council has taken many steps to open up engagement over the last eight years but could clearly do more.

Deliberative Democracy

Deliberative Democracy puts consultation and discussion at its core; it differs from traditional democratic theory in that authentic deliberation, not mere voting, is the primary source of legitimacy for the law. I strongly believe we need to increase the use of deliberative democracy in which genuine engagement and participation are central to decision-making. This means adopting and adapting elements of both consensus decision-making and majority rule.

Behind this argument lies the view that a small number of well-informed people will make better judgements than large numbers of ill-informed people. (Think Brexit if you need persuading.)

It will take a while to increase the political literacy of the many who've been sidelined completely in our current systems. Activities like the People's Budget and panels (as discussed in Chapter 5) are a step in this direction. Councils at all levels can put this at the heart of their strategy, both to make better decisions and to increase the support and engagement of the people.

Peoples' and Citizens' Assemblies

As it becomes clearer that the UK's national government is incapable of either representing or serving the people's interests, the call for opportunities to meet and discuss issues in Peoples' Assemblies' and larger-scale 'Citizen's Assemblies' has emerged.

Perhaps the best known example of Citizens' Assemblies is the Irish Government bringing groups of citizens together to inform decision making around the confrontational issues of gay marriage, legalisation of abortion and responding to climate change. This process involves 'sortition', familiar to us in the selection of a jury. It's not a totally random selection, as the process is carefully managed to give good representation across all relevant sectors of society. In the Irish work on reforming abortion law, 100 people met over five months to listen to a full range of expert inputs and views. Their final recommendations were not binding, but ongoing interaction with decision-making politicians, alongside the deeply authentic process, clearly impacted on the decisions made.

There are plenty of other good examples of these approaches such as the Mayor of Newham, Rokhsana Fiaz, who commissioned up to 16 People's Assemblies in a single month to bring ordinary local people into the Council's decision making. There are a plethora of organisations such as Involve and the Democratic Society that exist to support councils to take these steps.

In Frome we tried using random selection when creating the Neighbourhood Plan. However, we lacked the necessary expertise and consequently it didn't effectively bring in the voices of those not usually engaged. As Frome have declared Climate and Environmental Emergencies, there's huge potential to bring in a wide range of people via a Citizen's Assembly to help take responsibility for planning the actions needed to mitigate the looming disaster.

A word of warning: will our concerns at local level be listened to by the current national decision makers? According to the French academic Dominique Reynié, in early 2003, 36 million people across the globe took part in 3,000 anti war protests. The invasion of Iraq began on 20 March 2003. The evidence for elected government responding to moral pressure from the 'great unwashed', i.e. the common people, isn't great.

However, if government can recognise its need to listen for any reason – because of a genuine desire to do so, because it needs the votes of the assembled voice or because the pressure gets too great – then it may respond to local-level concerns. If they don't, then we need to start the process ourselves without buy-in from above.

The 'techno-fix'

At the root of our problem lies the fact that power is concentrated in the hands of the few, but can technology change this for us, the masses? There's an almost endless list of on-line platforms aiming to help the process of democracy like Loomio, Reddit and EBallot. However, at a local council level, the cost of such technology often rules out its use. At the moment, in the UK, the level of engagement at town level is usually along the lines of a Facebook poll. For example, Haswell Parish Council created a poll to gauge interest in a new community-based festival: 78% said 'Yes, I'd be interested' and 22% said 'No, I'm not interested'. This was very useful guidance in deciding to set up a festival. Frome regularly uses simple Survey Monkey polls to assist budget decisions.

My view is that while ensuring physical notice boards are kept up-to-date may still be the highest priority, I can see the increasingly important role technology can play in opening up participation.

Making democracy work for the majority

As central government's ability to provide anything significantly useful reduces, the list of organisations seeking to re-find democracy for the first time since the ancient Greeks is endless. Some organisations have funds to support local initiatives or may wish to carry out research. A selection from my list would include:

- The Co-intelligence Institute's 'Wise Democracy Project'
- The Democratic Society's 'Public Square'
- Simpol's the 'Voice for Global Solutions in Parliament', which works with 60 MPs
- More United, one of a number of cross-party political movements
- Together, also a cross-party movement, which calls itself a new network dedicated to reforming the UK's political system by putting more power into the hands of people and communities across the country.

Most of these are organisations ostensibly working to make democracy function. Bizarrely, many are government funded, despite the ruling parties aversion to open democracy. I would challenge whether they're really of anything other than passing interest to those of us engaged with doing things rather than talking about doing them. Perhaps I'm too cynical, but unless these organisations look to the community and offer practical ways to transfer power downwards, they may just be diverting energy from a democratic revolution.

4) Change the system

One could reasonably argue that it's not the place of a short book on how to make local-level government function better to engage in Big Ideas of total change. But I believe that within some substantially-radical approaches there are ideas from which we can learn. For example, the good people of Frome may not have the power or desire to convert the UK's political system to anarchy, but if an understanding of some anarchic principles helps engage wider sections of the public in politics, it's got to be worth exploring. If total change is not for you then skip to the end of this section.

The last decade has seen some real attempts to change the system. For example, the Occupy Movement had over 1,000 camps globally at its height, and the Indignados and the 15 Million movements that filled the squares of Spain all had similar grievances they articulated and addressed through participatory democracy and occupations of public spaces. While the Spanish movements have been moderately successful, other movements, especially in Egypt and North Africa, have led to significantly worse situations for the common person.

When the Icelandic Pirate Party was invited to lead a coalition government, change seemed likely to come from within. Poet Birgitta Jonsdottir, who co-founded the party, describes Iceland's Peoples' Constitution as a beautiful thing: *"It was the first time in history where a people had enshrined in their constitution the word sustainability, showing that ordinary people really cared for future generations and for the future of the species, unlike the rapacious governments they usually were under."*

The Peoples' Constitution was never ratified, which Birgitta puts down to their lack of capacity to change the underlying infrastructure: *"What you need to do very early on is make sure there is a transition of authority over infrastructure... If you don't have that, then the alternative is to replace the existing infrastructure with something else, if you do neither of these, then your revolution will fail. That's the big thing that we learned in Iceland."*

The previously-mentioned Alternativet party in Denmark share common core values with IfF in that both put forward values rather than a manifesto. They started as a movement, of which the party was only one element, but have since struggled by being forced to play into more 'normal' politics.

In the UK, The Alternative, a small but incredibly dedicated and informed group, continue to offer a virtual platform that helps feed progressive movements with positive ideas.

If movements and parties like these were in positions of real power, given their origins it seems likely they would support initiatives at a local level, where people had more say in the decisions that affected them. To date none of them have managed to scale up and really change the game at a fundamental level. And – surprise, surprise – my examples of real change have come from countries where forms of proportional representation can allow new ideas to emerge.

What these movements have in common is elements of anarchism. Anarchy is almost always wrongly represented as groups of men in black destroying property; it's become a word that mustn't be spoken when considering 'more serious' alternatives. However, Edward Abbey better described anarchism as 'democracy taken seriously'. I believe anyone looking to reclaim politics from the bottom up ought to spend time looking at the many different models of anarchy that have been tested over hundreds of years.

In fact, one of the first actions of IfF was called by some 'an anarchic act': in a direct action to expose the ineptitude of higher levels of government, a group of councillors tore up the inappropriate tarmac used to 'mend' paving slabs and replaced the original slabs – without asking anyone's permission first. Elsewhere in the world, people repair holes in the roads, most notably in Rome where Gruppi Artigiani di Pronto Intervento (Artisan Emergency Services groups) fix pavements, repaint zebra crossings and leave only a stencilled 'GAP'.

If large numbers of empowered citizens in a community took this approach, real change could be achieved in a short space of time. Perhaps then they'd feel more able to challenge, ask, lobby, and demand. This combined with a more open and supportive democratic structure could create the foundation for real change. It's well known that doing physical things plays a really important part in building change. There was certainly some physical action in Cheran in Mexico. Illegal loggers were plaguing the local area, with tacit council support, so the people waged an insurrection and declared self-rule in hopes of ridding themselves of the ills that plague so much of Mexico. Neighbourhood assemblies then selected a new non political council. Slightly more risky than replacing a few paving slabs when you live in a country that has 500 murders a week.

Sitting somewhere between the two, 'Autrement for Saillans' in France have entirely reformed local government. Elected officials work in teams with citizens, sharing the power. Issue-based commissions (something like Frome's Panels) define priorities, which are implemented by Project Action Groups, and an impressive 24% of the population participate in these groups.

These aren't huge, earth-shattering ideas, but they clearly fulfil the criteria of allowing people to improve their lives at an everyday level. I believe the mindset of 'don't ask, just do it' will, and should, increasingly be part of the mix.

This brings me to municipalism, sometimes also described as 'social anarchy', which is not strictly changing the system but a practical way for the many to take back control from the few.

"Municipalism is a rising force that seeks to transform fear into hope from the bottom up, and build that hope together."

Ada Colau, Mayor of Barcelona.

Municipalism is a term coined by Murray Bookchin, essentially home rule by the municipality. His daughter Debbie wrote: *"It returns politics to its original definition, as a moral calling based on rationality, community, creativity, free association and freedom. It is a richly articulated vision of a decentralized, assembly-based democracy in which people act together to chart a rational future. At a time when human rights, democracy and the public good are under*

147

attack by increasingly nationalistic, authoritarian centralized state governments, municipalism allows us to reclaim the public sphere for the exercise of authentic citizenship and freedom."

Municipalism demands we return power to ordinary citizens, that we reinvent what it means to do politics and what it means to be a citizen. True politics is the opposite of parliamentary politics. It begins in local assemblies and is transparent, with candidates put forward who're 100% accountable to their neighbourhood organisations. Candidates who're delegates rather than wheeling-and-dealing representatives. It celebrates the power of local assemblies to transform, and be transformed by, an increasingly enlightened citizenry.

This kind of politics is being articulated more and more vocally in 'horizontalist' movements around the world. In the factory recuperation politics of Argentina in which cooperatives restarted factories closed by economic collapse; in the water wars of Bolivia where the people have fought off privatisation, and in the neighbourhood councils that have arisen in Italy running in parallel to a dysfunctional state. These movements are creating a politics that meets human needs, that fosters sharing and cooperation, mutual aid and solidarity, and that recognizes that women must play a leadership role. Municipalism has been achieved in cities and towns globally from Jackson, Mississippi, to Valparaíso in Chile and Naples, Italy. In 2018 three out of the five most populated cities in Spain had mayors from this movement, and there are more than 100 such municipalist platforms globally as I write.

To include Frome's recent experiments in the same breath as most of these movements feels just a little fraudulent. Ours was never a 'People's Movement' with the same scope and ambition. But the work of the first IfF councils has provided a platform for something much more radical and more genuinely Municipalist. The seeds are there in an awareness of the need to further develop ways for people to listen to each other. Away from the anathema of adversarial politics and entrenched ideologies, in an atmosphere that celebrates our similarities over our differences, it may be possible for completely new approaches to politics to emerge.

Kris Fowler's MA dissertation comments: *"Learning from experiences in Frome, Barcelona and around the world, I contend that the municipality is the organisational scale best able to bring about a new economic logic for the transition to a sane, sustainable, free and compelling twenty-first century life through truly democratic and authentically political processes."*

As with other ideas I've introduced in this chapter, there's much more to say about municipalism and to explain how its central methodology could be useful for town and parish councils. Radical municipalism is a project to take direct democratic control over the places where we live. As more and more significant places achieve higher levels of autonomy, it leaves central government less and less space to mismanage. It's a way to build community and force elites to listen to demands at the same time.

The five town councils in Devon, which in 2019 became controlled by independents all operating with forms of Ways of Working, have significant potential to adapt and take on well tested ideas of municipalism, sharing their strength in numbers and taking greater control.

A word of warning: dark municipalism

The distance between the positive side of taking control of our own decisions and the negative is not great. For example, the Five Star Movement in Italy has been campaigning on a platform of direct democracy and environmentalism. In March 2018 they won the largest percentage of the vote in Italy and the most seats in parliament. Sounds good so far. Except that Beppe Grillo and Luigi Di Maio, the two foremost leaders of the party, have called for expelling all migrants from Italy and ending the flow of migrants to Europe. Following the 2018 elections they've entered into a coalition with the Far Right Lega Nord, a party advocating full regional autonomy and protecting the 'Christian identity' of Italy. Taking care of ourselves can have very different forms.

THE CONCLUSIONS
Frome

I've now come to the end of my role as a councillor with Independents for Frome. Initially, I wanted to be part of a parish council that punched above its weight and changed systems stuck in a previous century. My journey has revealed many things; most significantly, that the public are interested in the politics of where they live, just not the Westminster politics of confrontation. Also that it's possible to change the culture of a town council so that significant numbers of people come to meetings, engage and contribute and it's not that hard to extend this engagement into the wider community.

'Just' getting elected is not the end of the story. To effect significant change it takes a council and councillors who aren't afraid to change the traditional power relationship with the people. They must be up for far-ranging discussions about what their town wants to be and then to be ambitious and take risks to achieve these goals.

It turns out that the lowest levels of local government can raise significant sums of money to fund this ambition, by building capacity to fundraise, by borrowing and selling unwanted assets. Funds can also come directly from the people, who are generally happy to accept tax rises when they can see the need and feel the change. What we've done in Frome over the last few years is to play the role of a catalyst in supporting and empowering the community to be in a better place than it was. However, we shouldn't play down the challenges we face as austerity forces the town's strapline to become 'if we don't do it no one will'.

Is much of this known about by many residents in Frome? I don't think so; nor do I think this is crucial. Perhaps surprisingly given my earlier appetite for participation, I think we can get carried away worrying whether everyone is consulted or on board with every idea and decision. The direction towards greater engagement and involvement is at the core of IfF's achievements and should steadily grow, but there's also a need for leadership. The art is knowing which route to take and when.

Inspiring others

IfF has also played an important role as a 'first mover', taking risks, trying them out and sharing our successes and failures. I remain exasperated that we've largely had to do this ourselves. But there is now a wave of 'first followers', who're playing an incredibly important role in giving credibility to ideas and taking them to the next stage, (internet search 'first follower' on YouTube' to find a short video that brilliantly explains the role).

I see Frome as one building block in a vast network of communities trying to do things better. If I stand back a bit in time, the picture will emerge of the majority of local councils doing it for themselves.

Climate breakdown and the bigger picture

The area that first engaged me in local politics in 2010 was looming climate breakdown. I believe it's vital that we, both as individual towns and working together at a community level, develop a response to this emergency. At town council level this means two things: firstly, orchestrating projects that Frome Town Council describe as 'clean and healthy' and secondly, in supporting initiatives that help us prepare for a future that won't be as benign as the past.

I'm proud that in Frome people have wholeheartedly engaged with Extinction Rebellion's campaigns and that among the new 2019 councillors there were five arrests from climate actions in London. At the same time, there've been a series of actions at home looking to inform and engage rather than disrupt. This movement and these people, often supported by the town council, have been connecting to other towns throughout the region. I believe in the next few years solving the problem of climate breakdown will emerge as the area that trumps all others.

What next for IfF?

17 new IfF councillors have just started their work in Frome. I'm delighted none of them were in the original group of 2011 councillors, avoiding the risks of complacency that might have otherwise crept in. They're already bringing new energy and ideas. IfF, in its current form, is technically 'owned' by the existing councillors, it has no membership and no leaders. It does, however, have a good track record and masses of available experience. It will be for these new councillors to take the adventure where they, together with the people of Frome, want to go. Their challenge will be to avoid taking the first steps on what Aristotle saw as the inevitable route towards oligarchy and tyranny. By which I mean falling back on the familiar and becoming less ambitious, less risky and less participatory – looking inwards rather than outwards and serving their own needs rather than those of the broader community.

What we have in the UK is a pretence of democracy; what we've started in Frome has inspired more people to be drawn into making the decisions that affect their lives, which is closer to the 'rule by the people' society our Greek forefathers envisioned. I've always regarded this whole *Flatpack Democracy* process as an evolving experiment, and I'm extremely proud to have been at the party.

Perhaps I should leave the last word to Margaret Wheatley, who said: *"There is no power for change greater than a community discovering what it cares about."*

Appendices

■ *APPENDIX 1*

The Independents for Frome Ways of Working
"The noble art of losing face will one day save the human race." **Piet Hein**

These values and guidelines were drafted by the 17 independent individuals elected to Frome Town Council in May 2015. They are based on the original Ways of Working adopted in 2011.

Five Core Values
Independence. We will each make up our own mind about every decision without reference to a shared dogma or ideology.
Integrity. Decisions will be made in an open and understandable manner. Information will be made available even when we make mistakes, and everyone will have the opportunity to influence decisions.
Positivity. We will look for solutions, involving others in the discussions and not just describing problems.
Creativity. We will use new, or borrowed, ideas from within the group and the wider community to refresh what we do and how we do it.
Respect. We understand that everyone has an equal voice and is worth listening to.

We will adhere to these values by challenging ourselves and each other with the following:
- We'll avoid identifying ourselves so personally with a particular position that this in itself excludes constructive debate.
- We're prepared to be swayed by the arguments of others and to admit mistakes.
- We're willing and able to participate in rational debate leading to a conclusion.
- We understand the value of constructive debate.
- We accept that you win some, you lose some; it's usually nothing personal and there's really no point in taking defeats to heart.
- We'll maintain confidentiality where requested and agree when it will be expected.
- We'll share leadership and responsibility and take time to communicate the intention of and approach to the work we undertake.
- We'll have confidence in, and adhere to, the mechanisms and processes of decision-making that we establish, accepting that the decisions of the majority are paramount.

- We'll sustain an intention to involve each other and others rather than working in isolation
- We'll trust and have confidence and optimism in other people's expertise, knowledge and intentions. We'll talk to each other, not about each other.

■ *APPENDIX 2*

Job descriptions

Many, if not most, parish- and town-level councils have no job descriptions at all for their staff and/or the key roles councillors play. This lack allows in all kinds of ambiguity that can easily be taken advantage of, especially in relation to power and authority. The job descriptions shared below are intended to offer some guidance in relation to these posts. Depending on the size and ambition of any given council, they would definitely need to be adjusted and evolved to meet a specific situation.

The Town Clerk *(taken from the formal council standing orders)*
- Will brief the Leader on a weekly basis on the operational work of the council and issues within the town
- Will seek advice from the Leader when making significant decisions
- Will have their leave or time off in lieu agreed in advance by the Leader
- Will have their performance appraised at least annually, jointly by the Leader and the Mayor
- Will ensure the Leader is aware of any upcoming meetings with external organisations, and the Leader will do the same for the Town Clerk
- The Leader and Town Clerk will jointly consider the work programme and strategic documents on a monthly basis and jointly propose changes and additions to the council and/or the relevant committee.

Official Leader *(taken from the Standing Orders)*
The role of the Leader of the Council Leader of the Council will:
- Work with the Town Clerk and councillors to develop and propose to council the strategic direction and policy objectives of the council
- Will not alter the strategic direction of the council.
- Will work with the Town Clerk to ensure the strategic direction and operational management of the council are working effectively
- Will work with the Town Clerk to negotiate on behalf of the council with other local authorities and organisations in order to deliver the strategic direction and policy objectives

- Will discuss with the Mayor and relevant committee chairs the purpose of any negotiation and report the outcome to the council or the relevant committee
- Will be a member of all standing committees and the Senior Staff Advisory Group.

Official Leader *(taken from an internal and informal sharing to inform ifF councillors)*
- Will be a link from and to the Iff Group and senior management; 'this is the way we are thinking' kind of thing
- Will be a spur to action: oiling the internal wheels, providing some energy, adopting a 'just do it' attitude and generally staying optimistic
- Will act as Father Confessor to the Town Clerk and others, especially when things are going (or have gone) wrong – smoothing out wrinkles and keeping a tight hold on solutions
- Will come up with, or listen to, new ideas, getting a nod from others and introducing them into the system
- Will advise several staff on options
- Will provide confidence: 'Don't worry it'll work' or 'You must be joking'
- Will be a focal point for IfF issues, talking to individual councillors, providing advice and suggesting a course of action

The Mayor *(taken from Standing Orders)*
Roles and Responsibilities:

1) To act as a focus/figurehead or 'First Citizen for Frome'
- Open events in the community
- Judge competitions and award prizes
- Attend events as the town's representative
- Help to promote issues (not necessarily council issues but not contrary to council's policies)
- Raise funds for local charities.

2) To chair the council
Help to agree agendas, plan and prepare for council meetings. Chair full council meetings, in accordance with standing orders and to promote public engagement.
3) To act as spokesperson for council
- Give speeches
- Give interviews on behalf of the council to local and national media
- Maintain the Mayor's social media accounts with support from staff
- Write pieces for the local press (currently, but not necessarily, a weekly column)

Personal Specification
- You should be able to commit a significant amount of time to the role (between 2 and 16 hours a week)
- A basic general knowledge of the Frome community is really important. Specific knowledge of parts of the community can be helpful too.
- You should have experience of public speaking or a willingness to learn the skills required
- Ideally you would have a plan, idea or theme for your year as mayor.

You will need a level of political awareness/sensitivity (be aware of conflicts of interest, inappropriate endorsements etc).

Deputy Mayor *(taken from Standing Orders)*
To deputise in the absence of the Mayor, undertake any of the roles and responsibilities of the Mayor as needed. You might also want to have a plan or theme to enact – this must not contradict, and should ideally complement, that of the Mayor.

Other Committees
Frome Town Council adopted only two committees during most of 2011-2019. The roles of these can be found by an internet search. The chairs of these hold important roles as both have considerable delegated powers. The notes which follow describe the role, rather than making up a formal Job Description.

Town Matters Chair *(taken from an internal and informal sharing to inform ifF councillors)*
- Chairing bi-monthly meetings.
- Meeting the clerk a month prior to this to sketch out the agenda
- Reading all papers and preparing for the meeting, which may require further discussion with the town clerk
- Maintaining a watching brief on the work plan in relation to areas associated with the Town Matters remit. This may require meetings with relevant staff
- Involvement in staff management (employment and appraisal) in the areas covered by this committee
- Attending the Council Matters meeting and the Senior Staff Advisory Group.

The deputy should engage with setting the agenda, deputise for the chair and support the chair in meetings (which might mean acting as a devil's advocate role as well as straight supporting).

The Council Matters Chair *(taken from internal notes)*
This person chairs the bi-monthly meeting but has a role within the centre of the

council because the committee has direct staffing and financial responsibilities to:
- Provide vision and strategy.
- Monitor budget and spend (over and under).
- Oversee significant personnel matters, including appointment and recruitment
- Organise training and development programmes
- Monitors the effectiveness and efficiency of the council
- Track progress on Annual Work Plans
- Attend to councillor behaviour
- Is involved in health and safety
- Engage in the appraisals of senior staff
- Input into the updating of standing orders and procedures
- Has insight into agreements with other bodies, contracts and partnerships and the sale and purchase of land.

IfF Convenor *(taken from internal ifF notes)*
This person must facilitate the following:
- Arrange and agree calendar of meetings for the year (monthly)
- Book venues for meetings
- Send out regular reminders and requests for agenda items
- Produce and distribute monthly agenda
- 'Chair' regular IfF meetings.
- Keep a record of meetings/actions
- Distribute IfF minutes to the town clerk (after editing if necessary)
- Make sure actions and ideas put forward at meetings are collected and not forgotten
- Update IfF registration documents with electoral register (annually)
- Invite occasional guest speakers and relevant staff
- Help with arrangements for 'away days' and similar training opportunities
- May occasionally be required to act as a mediator in potential disputes and to take the 'temperature' of the group outside of meetings
- Troubleshoot
- Keep calm and smile a lot.

The Deputy Convenor will work with the Convenor to assist in the delivery of the above.

The chair of Planning Advisory Group (PAG) *(taken from internal ifF notes)*
As described elsewhere, in order to help clarify the role of the town council in planning decisions, the council replaced a 'Planning Committee' with an Advisory

Group. This group had a much clearer focus on the really significant recommendations Frome might make (given the lack of any direct decision making powers).

The role of the chair is to:
- Liaise with the planning manager to check for large, significant or potentially contentious planning applications prior to meetings
- Set an agenda with applications as above for discussion along with pre-app presentations, which may be in closed sessions before or after the PAG meetings
- Chair PAG meetings with back up from deputy chair on a three-week cycle
- Occasionally make representations to the Planning Board at the district
- Occasionally meet with developers, landowners and agents for informal pre-app discussions
- Aim to stay awake/abreast of planning policy at national and local level
- Be aware of housing and employment needs in town.

The role of a Sponsor

In order to help share roles and enable councillors to focus on their particular interests and expertise, the role of 'sponsor' was desi gned.

The Sponsor:
- Acts as the 'go to' person for their specified area so that staff/council/public has a point of contact
- Needs to have knowledge of, or a willingness to learn about, the area of their sponsorship
- Must engage with outside agencies and other councils/bodies/government to develop 'big picture' knowledge where relevant
- Should play a coordinating role in the community so that they develop signposting/consultation/engagement/meetings
- Should liaise with other relevant sponsors so there's a crossover, and build on work and ideas
- Should keep the council/staff and relevant parties informed
- Must work with relevant staff and be part of setting priorities
- Will attend relevant Senior Staff Advisory group meetings.

■ *APPENDIX 3*

Some thoughts from Mel Usher

Mel Usher instigated IfF and was behind much of the confidence and aspiration that influenced the way the group developed. Part of Mel's background was as chief executive of South Somerset District Council. He's spoken widely to groups of councillors and council staff. The following are notes he shared with me for one such talk he gave to the Society of Local Town Clerks.

Much has been written about Frome Council being independent. There is no denying that this has been crucial in how we select councillors, how we interact with one another and others and in some of the values we have adopted. However, something else is at play here that centres on a classic cultural change programme, despite never being called that.

Most of our travels and contact with other councils boil down to several common moans:
- The clerk doesn't understand/let us do what we think we should be doing
- The rules and procedures of the council and the law don't allow you to do this
- The councillors aren't tuned-in to modern local government and won't allow us staff to get on with the job
- We have always acted like this and it's been fine with us. Why change? What's wrong with what we have got now?
- The voters won't like this and I am elected to make this decision
- We have no money (often because there has been no attempt to raise the precept nor to explain why it is necessary)
- Our council is riven with factions and petty in-fighting on the political stage, so there is no consensus on what we should do next.

Of course, not every council is like this, it is a gross simplification, but few in the sector wouldn't recognise at least some of these traits in their home council. Whilst councils can receive help from NALC and elsewhere to solve knotty legal problems there is very little assistance around cultural change, partly because there are no accepted role models.

We are not advancing FTC as the only model; local circumstances and requirements will dictate how a council operates and that is right. However, there may be some mileage to some of these thoughts:
Ditch the Local Government Speak. Have you noticed how we suddenly adopt a new impenetrable language of our own when we write reports or enter a committee arena? We have tried very hard to rid ourselves of all of this.

Challenge Belief systems. It's absolutely crucial that as councillors (and staff) we ask the question 'Why?' Don't stop at the first reply to a 'Why', for example 'Because we have always done this'. That's not an answer! Keep going with, 'Why have we always done this?' In effect, each answer forms the basis of the next question until you get to the root of a problem; it might take as many as five 'whys'.

Be Nice. It's good to be different. Once you have carved out a niche, stick with it. People know what to expect from you. Our niches have been around saying 'yes', engaging with people, being a little odd and being independent.

Celebrate connections, be outward looking and seek diversity. There is a tendency for many providers of services to look inwards at their own efficiency. That's fine but it's not enough. Every community, big or small, has a myriad of voluntary organisations, informal one-off events, statutory services, local groups and delivery people. We've spent a lot of time identifying these people and helping them see connections, building their strengths and taking a holistic view. In theory, that should make all of our efforts more effective.

Look for expertise in unexpected places. Why do we sometimes assume that because we're elected we're the repository of all knowledge? Every community has a wealth of different experiences within it.

Create space for the unplanned and stay open-minded. Frome Town Council has a fairly sophisticated system of moving from strategy to work planning to implementation and then subsequently review. However, some of the best decisions we've made have been opportunistic, seeing the budget as a guideline rather than a blueprint.

Use resources as a tool for change. We see all of our staff and money as being a resource for change. Yes, much is locked up in year-on-year budgets, but you can create headroom. The level of the council's General Reserve is recommended at three months of running costs, for the right reasons you may wish to dip well below that.
Mix it up. Use skills and experiences at all different levels to the advantage of the community. Be prepared to move firmly away from the old roles in which the staff are there to wait until the councillors tell them what to do.

Make more mistakes. This is a difficult one to get across without being misrepresented. If you only do what you have always done and always err on the side of caution and safety you will never change, even though the world outside has moved on. The argument goes that by doing the same you will never make a mistake: 'it worked last year, so it will work again'. But this assumes that you are doing the right things in the first place… you could be doing the wrong thing right. So there is a school of thought that says if you are really pushing the boundaries you are bound to be at fault sometimes. Usually, when this happens there is a search for a 'victim' – 'who's to blame?'. We have tried to avoid this; if you don't, you can never really ask anyone to experiment with a new way of doing something. Staff members have left the council, but none for making a cock up.

Ready, Fire, Aim. Of course this is the reverse of normal business and government philosophy and does not apply in all cases, so use sparingly! There is, however, a tendency at a local level to overthink a problem, to delay a decision, to put things off and to over consult without any end product. Sometimes it's best to get started and learn as you go along even if you are still uncertain of the final objective. As long as you are heading in the determined direction, the exact point of arrival doesn't always matter too much.

Finally, a comment on legacy. The approach described above has developed over eight years. It is, of course, entirely vulnerable to the whim of voters. A different group of councillors in 2019 could change that direction completely. The town clerk has an interesting role in those circumstances. While their role is to carry out the wishes of the councillors, there is the opportunity to suggest where things have benefitted the public or the workings of the council.

From the start we put some things in place aimed at ensuring decisions would be long lasting. Most obvious of these is probably moving land acquired by the council into charitable trusts. Hopefully, this would make it harder for a new council, intent on short-term realisation of assets, to sell off such land.

Conversely, the councillors departing in 2019 have ensured all long-term funding arrangements are coming to an end, accepting it is the right and role of those about to be elected to make those decisions. We will deliberately leave a house very much in order, but one where new strategies and approaches can easily be enacted. Things may change and undoubtedly some should. As a councillor with one eye on legacy, I write with a certain hypocrisy, but I was very much part of tearing up the rule book in 2011!

Thanks

Flatpack 2.0 has drawn heavily on the thoughts and writings of others, for which I am most grateful. Primarily these have come from Mel Usher with additional contributions and wisdom from Jean Boulton, Toby Eliot, Max Wide. I'd also like to thank Kris Fowler for the offer of research which I took up with alacrity.

Peter Andrews' initial intention was to edit and publish the book. This evolved into research with other councils and then much more substantive creation and writing. Peter has said this will be his last book,, Whether he is able to stick to that or not, he is owed much by those of us into compost, as well as local politics.

In drawing together material for *Flatpack 2.0* we interviewed a number of people who hold key positions in councils who have headed down the route of reclaiming politics at a local level. It is always dangerous to name them, as some may feel missed out. I am grateful to everyone who took time to speak to us directly and a longer version of their thoughts will appear, in time, on the website. Thanks also to go to those who contribute to the group of elected and aspiring councillors that I and Pam Barrett of Buckfastleigh shepherd.

Peter Macfadyen

FLATPACK DEMOCRACY
A DIY GUIDE TO CREATING INDEPENDENT POLITICS

STILL AVAILABLE FROM ECO-LOGIC BOOKS

PRAISE FOR PETER MACFADYEN AND FLATPACK DEMOCRACY

We all sleep with *Flatpack Democracy* under our pillows.

Wells Independents

... many thanks for the inspiration that has enabled us to clear out the dead wood here!

Portishead Independents – P. G.

...this all started because three of us were having a chat on the school run about problems at the Council and what could/should happen. Then we found *Flatpack* (thanks!), then we found our candidates then we all got elected. Sounds so simple, eh?! Not been an easy ride, but glad we stuck with it.

Hadleigh Together – S. A.